When Water Was Free

An Urban Commentary from an
East Texas Front Porch ©

Written by
Patrice K. Walker

Edited by
Joan Burke Stanford

Sis Cass -
You are such an
inspiration.
Thanks -
Patrice Walker

SimDen Publishing
1515 Town East Blvd
Suite 138-104
Mesquite, TX 75150

ISBN 0-9758948-0-3

Contributors:

Joan Burke Stanford, Editor

Candace Cottrell, Cover Designer

Deneen Jones, Page Creator

Rev. Alton R. McKinley, Biblical References

Pastor Terry M. Turner, Father in the Faith
Founder and Senior Pastor-Mesquite Friendship Baptist Church

All biblical references contained in this book are adapted from the King James Version of the Holy Bible.

All stories related to this book are true, but certain names have been changed to protect the privacy of the people mentioned.

Special Sales:

Book clubs and groups wishing to purchase 10 or more copies of the book should contact the publisher directly for special pricing.

First edition

Dedications:

To the greatest daddy who ever lived, Leonard Clifton Kissentaner. Thank you for being such a great friend.

To the sweetest mommy God ever made, Naomi Emmaline Kissentaner. I want to be just like you when I grow up.

Acknowledgments:

Jordan and Jamie, my two lovely daughters, this is for you. I don't know if I will ever write another book, but this one is written with you both in mind. After the death of your father, you were left without a history of his childhood, his family memories, his struggles, victories, or his personal memories with you. This prompted me to begin journaling my thoughts into this book, just to share more of me with you.

You'll get a glimpse of my childhood, and learn even more about how life's lessons have shaped me into who I am. You'll see how and why I value family and marriage. You will also see how much fun I had as a child. Hopefully, you will also be able to identify unhealthy relationships, and learn how to walk away from them, with no regrets. I have learned my greatest lessons by paying attention to the people, places, things, and ideas around me. You two have taught me in ways you won't understand until you are parents yourselves. The final chapter of this book is my love letter to you, as you embark on life as maturing young ladies.

Certain parts of the book are comical; others offer a vicarious look at a simpler lifestyle; while other chapters were more difficult to write because of the heartfelt emotions involved. However, the difficult chapters contain the greatest lessons. My prayer remains that as you become mature women, you will be able to understand all that is contained herein, and you will enjoy reading the book as much as I have enjoyed writing it.

This dedication is written as Jordan prepares to go to New York City to compete against models from all over the world, at the age of twelve. Jamie is preparing for another stellar track season in the 400 meter run. If neither of you ever win another competition, that's okay by me. You've won the prize already. You've captured my heart and my undying love for you, forever. I thank God that He chose me to be your "Mom." You make me proud every day, even when you get on my last nerve.

I live each day recalling what the Great Emancipator once said, and I agree with his words:

"It is not important who my ancestors were, as it is who my children become."

-Abraham Lincoln

I may never become a celebrity, and I will never be perfect; but I will always be your mother. I love you.

-Mom

With special thanks:

To my loving husband, Bernard my new sixteen-year-old son, Geoffrey.

To my brother, sister, and my other heavenly co-authors whose roles in my life make this story the wonderful account that it is.

To Sharon Ewell-Foster, my best-selling author cousin. Thanks for encouraging me to write.

To Twanna Williams, thanks for daring me to do it.

To Alicia, Tanya and Sytonia for the wonderful childhood friendship. LYLAS

To supportive friends, Sonji, Carla, Cazandra, Phyllis, Lawren, Pamela, Jeretha, Mischelle and Melissa; when I shared with you what I was about to undertake, each of you encouraged me. Some of you have witnessed the storms in my life, and reverently stood there with me as I went through them; others have come along later in my life, but all of you have encouraged me to "press toward the mark" and finish the book. Thanks for your love and support, and for telling me how proud you are of me.

To Rita Curington and Elaine White, my two high school English teachers who identified my gift of writing long before I knew of it.

To my extended family, "The Tribe of Jordan"...there's not another group of people anywhere else quite like you — anywhere. Thank God! And to the Kissentaners and Ewells, my daddy's family; much love to all who bear the name.

To everyone mentioned in the book, the fact that you are in my life is a wonderful story worth sharing with the world.

To Betty & Labron Walker, my new parents. I'll never consider you in laws. You are my second set of parents. I am honored to be a part of your family.

To my church family at Mesquite Friendship Baptist Church, the best church this side of heaven; I love you for loving me and accepting me as the imperfect vessel that I am. Pastor Turner, keep on preaching!

To you, the reader…I dedicate this book to you and pray that your emotions will identify with my emotions, as you journey through these pages from Athens, Texas, all the way to heaven.

Last and most important, "To God be the glory for the things He has done."

My prayer is that He is pleased with what I have done, and that someone who is in distress has smiled; someone who was puffed-up has been broken; someone who was grieving now believes; someone who refuses to let go, will let God. I did!

CONTENTS

Prologue 2003

Parched from the intense Dallas, Texas July heat, I merged my car onto Central Expressway, and I thought to myself how I should choke the salesman who sold me this car with black leather seats. Traffic was moving, but not as quickly as I needed it to. My "old school" radio station just wasn't doing it for me. Despite how good Earth Wind & Fire's "Love's Holiday" sounded, the fact remained; it was hot! My air conditioner was kicked down to 60 degrees, and that still wasn't doing the trick. The dashboard thermostat registered 111 degrees, and I believe it was every bit that hot. To make matters worse, I had overbooked myself for three appointments and was burdened to choose which one I'd make. The choices were getting a much-needed retouch on my perm, going to my daughters' school to meet the new PTA president, or running by my husband's job and picking up a letter to mail. Due to the urgency of the letter, and the sweetness of the man I'd have to pick it up from, I maneuvered my car into the exit lane to take the Knox-Henderson off ramp. Besides, my hairdresser Quin always knows that I'm usually about seventeen minutes late for my appointments. But that's okay; we have an understanding. Plus, I don't mind waiting around at the shop if she ever needs to "work someone in," from time to time. So, I dialed her number on my new camera phone, and let her know that I'd be late, as usual. She laughed with her trademark Minden, Louisiana chuckle and told me to take my time. That's why I love her. She's always accommodating, and *always* giggling.

As I hung up, my eyes witnessed the worst mess my little mind could handle on that blistering summer day. There it was, just as you probably suspected, the biggest traffic jam ever. In that part of the city, it's quite normal to have one woman driving a convertible two-seater Jaguar collide with another woman driving a Bentley. It's my estimation that they must be too busy counting their money to drive. They'll get out of their car, with their Yorkshire terrier in tow, call their corporate executive husbands, and have *him* talk to the police, *for them*. They will hug each other good-bye and that's it. No fighting, no cursing, no accusations…just big money, big cars and big hugs leading to big traffic.

Today was no different. I had the pleasure of watching this newest reality program unfold before me. Mrs. Other-Color-Rich-Woman swerved to miss a piece of metal in the street and was hit by Ms. I-Took-His-Benz-And-The-Bentley-And-I've-Never-Been-Happier-Since-The-Divorce. From their pleasant conversation, I could only assume they must have known each other, possibly from some stuffy bridge party, maybe from lunch at the country club, or perhaps a "Mom's day out" at the spa.

They couldn't have been in a rush to get anywhere, because everyone living in Highland Park owns the city. So, I can't imagine what happened.

Well, let's just put it like this; by the end of the day, somebody's news station would get the story, and the police department would waste taxpayer money trying to track down who left the piece of metal in the street. Meanwhile, I tried to imagine what it must feel like to afford a Bentley. I couldn't fathom owning a car valued at more than a city block in my hometown. I found the whole thing rather amusing. Anyway, such is life in the big city.

Obviously late for all three appointments, and extremely frustrated, I stopped at a convenience store to get out of the intense heat, and to grab something cool to drink. No soda, no juice, and certainly no beer, just water. I waited patiently in line, as did the five others in front of me. When the clerk smiled, and, in a Middle Eastern dialect, asked me for "One dollar vifty sehben cents." I mistakenly peered over my shoulder looking for whomever he had rung up out of turn. After all, I was only buying water, and he couldn't have been talking to me. So, I thought to myself, *Exactly what is the man behind me buying?* By then, the clerk smiled again and said, "Umm, so sotty Miss, you water one dollar vifty sehben cents."

{Please press PAUSE} Author's note: From time to time, I will ask you to mentally press Pause to ponder a situation, or to think about a few things. So, here's one: please press Pause, while I contemplate kindly giving this man his water back. {Press PLAY, please.}

For a moment, I left the planet. How could something that someone had drawn off the tap, just like I do, cost almost two bucks? What is that bottle made of anyway, diamonds?

Better yet, I must have missed the sign out front because apparently this was a misnamed Neiman Marcus convenience store I stumbled into.

Obviously, they don't know I'm not from this part of Dallas. I live in Mesquite, but I'm from Athens, Texas, home of the world famous black-eyed pea jamboree, the highly disputed home of the first hamburger, where pecan (pronounced PUH' kahn, not pea can) trees grow tall in everybody's yard, and I know where real water comes from. It comes from Lake Athens or the Rohrer Spring near Eustace. Don't believe me? Just ask one of the major bottlers today. They'll tell you I'm right because that's where their bottled product comes from.

I thought to myself, *I'm not paying that much for water,* while feverishly digging for more money in my fake Fendi bag. *Who do they think I am?* It must be the car; they think I've got money. Well, they are sadly mistaken. I'm just a middle-aged black woman who just happened to get a great deal on a great car. (Now, I'm wondering if the deal was really so great. Who, in their right mind, wants to bake in the summer heat for $529 per month?) It was a great deal because nobody else wanted the Japanese portable microwave *oven*! I now remember that I bought the car in March, while the weather was cool. I should have kept my Altima and my big bag phone from 1990. (In those days, it was fashionable to walk around with a seven-pound bag of telephonic hardware on your hip.)

Anyway, I kept digging until I found the exact change to pay for the water, and I headed for my Lexus GS oven. Forget buying gas. I couldn't afford it *and* water.

Still reeling from the cold-water-in-my-face experience, I cranked the car, and headed back onto the freeway. While sitting behind the H2 Hummer strategically parked in front of me on the freeway, I smiled as I drove by Mrs. Rich Woman and the newly crowned 2003 Divorce Court Grand Prize Winner. I should have asked them for some more water money. Instead, I graciously smiled and shrugged my shoulders as I drove by, as if to say, "How could anyone be so careless, leaving that in the road for you, with all of your husband's belongings, to swerve and hit another driver?"

As I sipped my water, I thought back to a simpler time in my life, when there were no Hummers, no camera phones and certainly no bottled water. A day's work was free of e-mails. Plasma was something in your blood, and not the description of a television screen. The only traffic jam was caused by children running home from the bus stop. And the best therapy around came from the front porch of your parent's home. Remember that? I certainly do. That was when water was free.

Grab yourself a bottle of water, and join me on my mother's east Texas front porch swing, won't you? Climb the two steps and sit down. There's plenty of room on the porch, if you don't care for the swing. Be careful not to move Mama's cordless phone or her fly swatter. And whatever you do, please don't move her glass of water. She likes them just where she put them. After all, she is the mayor of Massey Street and her front porch is her office. You wouldn't go into your mayor's office moving his or her stuff around, now would you?

Introduction

Philosophically speaking, many may think that at the age of thirty-six, I am too young to write my memoirs. Besides, such writing is reserved for the rich and famous, right? Plus, memoirs have all of those rules of grammar, punctuation and etiquette to follow. Well, this book doesn't. However, for all of you English teachers who may read this and gasp at my disregard for the literary standards of usage, please note: I know the rules. Mrs. Curington, my senior high school English teacher, did a great job explaining participles, direct and indirect objects, and diagramming sentences. I paid attention, and I promise, I remember what she taught me. Despite what you may think, Mrs. C placed into my literary hands, a pretty good grasp of the English language. But this time, I'm loosening my grip.

This is *my* book, and since 1967 some of my life's experiences have not always allowed for perfect English. So, I ain't promising that everything will be grammatically correct. While speaking from the front porch, punctuation, capitalization, and grammatical rules don't necessarily apply. Moreover, if Shakespeare could get away with writing in an ancient foreign language, and still be recognized as one of the fathers of literature today, the literary world can tolerate a few "ain'ts," "fixings" and other small slices into the King's English. By George, I must be on the right track. Here are a few words you may stumble upon during our Massey Street conversation:

1. Finta - about to; preparing to. "I'm finta eat dinner."

2. Ret ta - ready to; preparing to leave. "I'm ret ta go."

3. Gon' - are going to. "How you gon' say that?" "How you gon' act?"

4. Funelize - the act of having a funeral. "They gone funelize him tomorrow."

5. Sehh- say (pronounced like Seth without the "t") "Whatchu sehh?"

6. Big ole- extremely large. "She had a big ole bowl of ice-cream."

7. Aw naww- expressed disapproval (spoken quickly, often accompanied with an index finger shake, and a side-to-side head turn.) "Aw naww, somebody done told you wrong!"

8. Hole up- hold up, pardon me. "Hole up, where y'all going?"

9. Ignut-void of knowledge. "She doesn't know any better, she's just ignut."

Possibly the most helpful tips to you, the reader, are as follows:

- Don't confuse the previous glossary of terms with Ebonics. This is east Texan we are speaking, for the sake of the learned.
- Don't waste your time trying to analyze this too much.
- Don't immerse yourself in futile summarization studies of "what the author was trying to say." The author is perfectly capable of saying exactly what is on her mind.
- Don't "read between the lines." What is printed on the lines is enough.
- In order to fully understand this book, you've gotta understand me. You've gotta see what I've seen and feel what I've felt. You've gotta come with me on this retrospective journey.
- Prepare yourself. Not everything you read will be politically correct. But then again, that's an oxymoron. If something is political, it's hardly ever correct.

So, as Shakespeare would write, "Backeth to the storieth." Or as my new father would say, "You burnin' day light, state ya bidness and let's go!"

Now, back to this rich and famous thing. Well, you, the reader, may now consider yourself honored to have read the work of the uncommonly rich and famous person because *I am rich*. Though my bank account will never reveal my true wealth, I am rich in love, joy, peace, and humor, according to my personal character account. This is the one account that I own that cannot be depleted or overdrawn, unless I alter my standards of excellence for myself. I am the account manager, and decide all deposits and withdrawals. When situations seem above my threshold of tolerance, I can withdraw some character from it, in the form of any fruit of the spirit, love, joy, peace (or humor), apply it to that circumstance, and clear the current hurdle.

Memoirs for the rich and famous? I am famous, to those who know me. Have I ever met the president? No. More importantly and correctly stated, "Has the president had the pleasure of meeting me?" The answer to both questions is "no." But my brother met, and actually traveled with the president when Bush was the governor of Texas. So that should count for something, right?

Have I met Cedric the Entertainer? Yes, and I like him better than any president who could ever be bought, oops, I mean voted into office. More importantly than either of those, I have personally met God. I had known of Him for a long time. I had read of Him in awesome stories, sang praises to Him, and recited rehearsed prayers to Him all of my life. I even gave gifts at Christmas in honor of the birth of His son. I finally met *The Great I Am*, for myself, three years ago on Christmas Day 2000. You'll read more about that in a later chapter.

At any rate, at the risk of sounding too far out of my league, I'm not calling this my memoirs because this work is simply my story. It's important that you understand that this is not a self-help book, not at all. It may be considered inspirational, but if you need help, I urge you to put this book down and try reading God's word first. Then, come back to this for a little entertainment, and some "front-porch psychology."

This story is...well... it's just me and the joyful, yet troublesome, wacky and wonderful, bitter and sweet, restful and stressful, submissive and rebellious, tried and true experiences I've had during this, my short sojourn on this planet.

Considering the Bible only gives us "three score and ten years," which in plain English equates to seventy years, my life is half over. So, I think it is best that I quickly get to work on something that hopefully will outlive me. If my life were a basketball game, I'd be at halftime, heading for the locker room to discuss strategies for the next half. My coach would go over what went well in the first half, what I could have done differently and what I did that really didn't work at all. In the final chapters of the book, we'll review what the coach had to say.

In the Bible, Methuselah lived for 969 years. That's about all my Bible says about him, other than he had children, and was the grandfather of Noah, the world's first cruise director. In 969 years, it doesn't mention him helping anyone, sharing with or caring for anyone, or feeding anyone. Nope. It just says he lived, had children, and then he died.

Death is no stranger to my family, so I aspire not to just "live." Death weaves in and out of my family at will, and always without permission. Nonetheless, we realize that death has no power of its own, and is only carrying out a mission directive from God. With that understood, death's pain to my family has been numbed by the soothing balm of assurance that it is only an order from God to take his children to their eternal homes.

These thirty-seven years, but more specifically these past three years, have taught me, the hard way, to appreciate and love each day from sunrise to sunset. I want to make each day I live count for something. I strive to make a positive difference in at least one thing that I do each day. My goal is to do a little bit better each day, just a tad better than I did the day before.

I don't care to waste another day trying to prove myself to anyone, trying to heal the world's problems, or trying to take others' matters into my own hands. There's one simple answer to all of those problems: God.

Somewhere between 1967 and 2002, I became a busybody, and wanted every thing and every body to be happy. I proudly wore the title "Busybody of the Millennium." I competed in a one-woman decathlon. Your problems were my problems. Your issues were my issues. Your struggles were my struggles. My house was your house. I was involved in too many people's lives, while mine crumbled underneath my busy feet. I tried to solve everyone's problems. I gave advice. I gave money. I gave myself. All along, I should have given the word of God, which is free and never runs out. My great advice soon faded because it wasn't necessarily always scripturally based, but was often filled with emotion and opinion.

You know what else happened? My money ran out, even though I was tithing. The needs of others overwhelmed my means. I knew I was doing the right thing by helping those in need, but I couldn't stop. However, I did it all with a clear conscience and a pure heart. "Give and it shall be given unto you, good measure, pressed down, shaken together and overflowing shall men give unto your bosom (Luke 6:38)."

My mistake was in believing that those same people would be the ones to give unto *my* bosom. Not so. Now, three wiser years later, I know that my duty is to my church, and it is the church's duty to help the needy, not mine. (The Bible teaches about bringing all the tithes into the storehouse. Funny, it failed to mention the poor house.) I apparently misunderstood.

I lost even more money after Sept. 11, totaling in the five digits — high five digits, a few dollars away from six digits. By giving so much of myself to others, I lost my identity in everyone else's woes. It didn't take long for me to come unraveled, as I soon did. So, God called a time-out for me. He sent me to a corner to sit down, shut up, and sort out exactly what I was doing, and to determine who and what was most important.

Now, spiritually renewed and ready for the second half of the game, I'm preparing for the final half of my life, knowing very well that I will still fall short from time to time.

But now, I more quickly recognize my errant ways, and I'm swift to ask for forgiveness over and over again (because I mess up quite frequently). I seek God's forgiveness when I'm guilty of intervening, and trying to help the sovereign, omnipotent, omnipresent, omniscient God to fix someone else's situation or my own. I have learned that He really doesn't need my assistance. It's just the busybody in me. Old habits do die hard.

The greatest purpose for this book is to fulfill my desire for my posterity. I want my daughters to be able to pick up this book in fifty years and hear my voice. Through these written words, I want the generations that come after my daughters', their children and their children, to read about my life and laugh with me, cry with me, and learn from me. That's the whole purpose.

If I make a few new friends from this book, that makes this writing journey even sweeter. If I can make a few people laugh their way through their seemingly tough situation, God gets the glory. If I can help anyone realize that they can make it, if they want to, then these days spent in front of my laptop, arranging my thoughts onto this blank canvas, will all be worthwhile. If through my experiences with the deaths of four very dear family members, I can help others to accept God's will, I will have completed the task assigned to each believer in 1 Thessalonians 4:13-18.

However, if along the way, I offend someone, or even worse, if I make a few enemies, that's very unfortunate. That is not my hope, but I'm no dummy. This is 2004. People are often offended by a little bit of anything, especially the truth. Although the Bible teaches, "The truth shall make you free," today, it's more like, "the truth shall make you fight." Hardly anybody wants the truth, especially when it takes us out of our comfort zone. But for once, I'm telling my story the way I see it, from my perspective. This solitary viewpoint comes from how I've viewed life while being tucked in this earthly bodysuit for these years. Some of it is funny, and some of it will possibly touch your heart and your box of facial tissues. Other parts will warrant a pause for thought, while other passages may provoke anger.

The people and situations are true. I've only changed a few characters' names to respect their privacy. If someone disagrees with *my* story, I encourage them to write their version of my story and hopefully people will read both accounts. Perhaps, if I have indeed offended or made an enemy; I will have provided an excellent stream for that person to get filthy rich, hopefully through the sale of his/her/our books. {Press PAUSE} I'm only kidding, okay? Let's have some fun with this. {Press PLAY}.

Goofy, witty, out of control, my *missed* calling, are terms and phrases used to describe one of my greatest assets – my sense of humor. This is but another gift from God, (straight from both my parents), but it has gotten me through some rather bizarre and difficult situations. When others who are more serious about life would have probably thrown in the towel, I have found that if I can laugh at myself, I can laugh about anything, and life becomes just a little bit easier to deal with.

I find it difficult being around people who are so serious about everything that they cannot relax and crack a stony face to smile. For instance, people who can't smile without pointing out a flaw in somebody else, while not recognizing their own maladies make me sick. They remind me of "splinters and beams" as recorded in the gospel of Matthew 7:1-5. I'm also not too fond of people who are so caught up into *self* and are so afraid of failing that they can't stop to laugh at a mistake they have made. (The proud; that's one of the six things God hates, according to Proverbs 6.) It's those people who should come to our front porch conversation and take a seat right next to Mama on her swing: the stiff necked affluent; the bourgeois (pronounced boosh zwha); the "Super Saints" (those who would lead others to think they have taken the express lane to righteousness and were born saved and have conquered all sin); and of course, the ignut.

All of these people make up a population Mama describes like this: "Honey, their wisdom teeth were pulled too early; they're just ignut. And the world is full of 'em. They're real easy to pick out in a room full of people, and most of 'em can't help it 'cause they don't know it."

While conversing on my mother's front porch, you will bear witness to some other pretty remarkable things that will make you want to laugh out loud, or at minimum, chuckle a bit.

Some may inquire, "Patrice, what makes you, qualified to write a book?" Do you have a degree in English? Journalism? A celebrity endorsement? Once again, the answer to all of those inquiries is a sincere no.

This story is about a girl from east Texas, armed only with a high school diploma, a steadfast faith in God and tons of mother wit. She has traveled the world, marched in the

Macy's Thanksgiving Day Parade, appeared on the news in Nice, France, was married to an officer in the U.S. Army, experienced life as an officer's wife; had the pleasure of having lunch with Ronald McNair (the African American astronaut who perished in the Challenger Space Shuttle disaster in 1986), worked with the U.S. Secret Service to book an international president coming to visit the United States, managed a multi-million dollar travel budget for a controversial faith healing televangelist, and taught collegiate classes, all without having a formal degree. That's what makes me qualified. To ask the question what makes me qualified to write my story is not the right query…it's *who* makes me qualified, and we both know who that is, right? I am just one of many ordinary women with extraordinary stories. My life has never been boring, and nobody can tell my story quite like I can.

What I do have is faith and who I do have is the God of Moses and David on my side. Moses, whose speech pattern was flawed, did not own a handheld Red Sea Opener, (Blackberry PDA) as he approached the shores of the unforgiving water. Instead, he stretched out what he had in his hand, and God did the rest. This book is being written with the same intestinal fortitude that I call "The Moses Initiative." I'm simply using what God has placed in my hands to do his work, and possibly pull off another modern day miracle. There are a few people who need to hear about Him, from somebody who is a faithful believer; however, not so "churchy" that they become saintly sickening. There are others who may need to know that everyone's ministry is not from the pulpit or from a syndicated television show. No, I'm not a "Super Saint." I'm a former travel industry veteran; mother of three children, struggling to pay bills just like everyone else. However, I have a special gift of writing, and interesting life stories that I have been called to share with others, most importantly my children.

David had only a rag and a rock in his hand, and he slew a killer twice his size, twice his age and twice his stature. That's all. I believe in that same God, and recognize that those things only occurred when God ordained them, in His perfect timing, not David's. He was only a kid, the baby brother, tending the sheep. However, when the adversary "called him out," he stood firm, ready to fight.

I have yet to have an undergraduate degree conferred to me, but I do hold the Master's degree in life. I've read its handbook, and know more now about how to survive in peace. Though I may have not passed every test as well as others, I remain in the course, desiring to learn more, ultimately reaching higher heights.

"The race is not given to the swift, nor to the strong, but to the one that endureth until the end."

Let's go to Athens. You've *got* to meet my family!

Chapter

1 "Who Am I"

I am the youngest of three children born to my mother. She had two children, Jerri Jane and Reuben, from a previous marriage. My father (the handsome rapscallion you'll meet later) had a son from a previous relationship. Jane, Rube and Daddy are all in heaven now, watching over me, and helping me to write this book. They remind me of the little things that otherwise may slip my mind.

I didn't grow up with my sister and brother at home because they were twenty-three and twenty years older than me, respectively. By the time I came along, they were long gone, and married with children. But I loved them, and hanging out with them was cooler than cool. So, I grew up as an only child, for a while, at least.

My parents were *very mature* when I was born. I can't say they were old, but they were more experienced than others having children at the time I was born. My mother was in her late thirties, and my father was in his early fifties, when the stork delivered the bouncing baby girl to them on a cool spring morning in May of 1967. Daddy was often mistaken as my grandfather and as Mama's daddy. It was pretty funny to him.

At the age of two, I could spell my entire name G-E-O-R-G-I-A P-A-T-R-I-C-E K-I-S-S-E-N-T-A-N-E-R. There are some adults who *still* can't spell my name, and there are days now, when I still struggle with it. My new married name is Walker, which is so much easier for people to say. Over the years, my maiden name has been hacked to pieces, and I've been called everything from Blassingame to Kennicott. But it's Kissentaner, pronounced KISS en tann er. It's pretty easy to say; it just looks intimidating.

I think a good place to start this journey is by sharing the details of the first and only time I ever skipped school. Let's roll back time to 1973.

After my first year as a kindergarten scholar in the Athens Independent School District, I realized school was overrated. I mean, it was okay, but I didn't get what all the hoopla was about. But at six years old, I agreed to keep going until something better came along. The truth is, I wasn't impressed. They didn't have anything at school that I didn't have at home. Old people, pencils, paper, lunch, swings; why did I need to go to school? The one redeeming factor for South Athens Elementary was the oatmeal cookies. They kept me going back. I'm convinced. The cooks at my school were the best in town.

{Author's note: In Athens, you can always tell what section of the city you are in by the name of the elementary school nearest you; South, North, West and Bel Air.} In many urban areas, you hear of the African American population residing on the "South side," but not so in Big A. We lived on the north side of the tracks. Yes, the tracks served as the great divide. The United States recognizes the Rocky Mountains as the separator between east and west. We had the tracks, which divided our city geographically, racially and socio-economically. You don't have to guess who lived in Bel Air, on the south side.

Each morning, Daddy and I would get up, get dressed and head to Daylight Donuts for our special time together. Two glazed donuts and chocolate milk was my routine. One morning in particular, as I slurped the last of my milk through the crazy straw, he mentioned, "Next Friday morning, I'm going to Dallas, but I'll be back home in time to pick you up from school."

Licking the glazed sugar crystals from my sticky fingers, I said, "Aww, Daddy, I wish I could go." Meanwhile, in my mind I thought, *You're not going to Dallas, without me!* We finished our breakfast and he dropped me off at school. I kissed him and like he did each morning as I closed the door, he said, "Make me proud, Sport!"

I was headed to Mrs. Smith's class. I really liked her. She was young and cute, and kept first grade interesting for me, despite my desire to help her teach the class. Even though I liked her, I liked my daddy more, and somehow, I was going to have to outthink both of them, so I could make the trip to Dallas with my "Road Dog."

After a few hours of reading Tip and Mitten, and using crayons and construction paper, I crafted my scheme for next week's day off, and planned it out in detail. I hoped it would work.

That night at dinner, while Mama and Daddy talked among themselves, I built up the nerve to announce, "We don't have school next Friday," while shoving cornbread into my mouth and looking pretty clever.

Mama answered, "You don't?"

"No Ma'am," I replied with jaws still full of cornbread.

"Patrice," she interrupted, "If I've told you once, I've told you a jillion times not to talk with your mouth full. Now chew that food up, *then* talk." (People with bad table manners wracked her nerves, and still do, today.)

I took a good slurp of Kool-Aid and wiped my mouth with the back of my hand to say, "Sorry, Ma, but there's one of those teacher's things next Friday and we don't have school."

While I sat there, my eyes danced back and forth like watching a ping-pong match as each of them spoke. Hoping they fell for it, I remained quiet. Mama and Daddy continued to discuss options for childcare for me. I thought to myself, *At least they believed me. I must be pretty smart. This is easy, and they are pretty silly.*

Without hesitation, Daddy spoke up, "Don't worry about it Baby, she can go with me. We'll just spend the day together. That way, I won't have to rush back home to pick her up. How 'bout that, Sport?"

I silently laughed to myself because they actually bought this bill of goods I peddled. My daddy, the smartest man on earth, just confirmed for me that parents were really goofy. I tricked 'em! Parents are easy to fool. Boy that was easy. I was very proud of myself. The hardest part of the trick was containing my excitement for another week, without spilling the beans.

Sure enough, Friday morning finally came. Mama had to be at work at seven, but she had already ironed my shirt and jeans and laid them neatly at the foot of my bed. I was awake when she told Daddy, "Just let her sleep a little later, today, since she doesn't have school."

I kept my eyes tightly closed, hoping she wouldn't notice me. (You do know that if you keep your eyes closed, people can't see you, right?) My book, my story, and at six years old, that's what I thought.

I envisioned the scene I had seen so many times before. She kissed Daddy on the cheek and zipped around the table gathering her things for work. I don't know why she always rushed. She only worked a half-mile from the house, and was the Director of Nurses, so she was the boss. Oh yeah, it's what they used to call "work ethics." Daddy held the door open for her, as she darted through reminding him, "Call me before you leave so I'll know y'all are on the road."

I opened my eyes just in time to see as Daddy pulled Mama back into the kitchen one more time to kiss her before she left, and it was one of those gross ones. Yuck! For a few minutes longer, I quickly closed my eyes again and tried to continue my sleeping charade, but the thought of them kissing made my stomach hurt.

I heard the familiar "clink, clink, clink" of Daddy's spoon as he stirred his coffee. The aroma of Maxwell House coffee still coated the air. I could even hear the coffee percolating through the glass thingamabob on top of the pot.

I finally crawled out of the bed, continuing my Academy award-winning act. As I stood there in the doorway in my Sesame Street pajamas, Daddy picked me up and whirled me around until Bert, Ernie, Big Bird and I were fully awake.

"How 'bout some coffee, Madame?"

"Sure thing," was always my comeback, whenever he asked me something.

He poured each of us a half cup of hot coffee, and we counted our heaping teaspoons of sugar together. One…Two…Three…Four and a pinch. Then he'd fill the rest of the cup with milk. (Daddy strictly followed the rule of never drinking anything darker than your skin. He never drank Coca-Cola, Dr. Pepper or root beer. It was always an orange soda or a Sprite.) This morning, what we drank actually tasted more like a coffee flavored hot milk shake. But boy, it was good!

As we sipped on our coffee, he read the morning news, and pointed out a few stories of interest to him. "What about some breakfast, Babycakes?" he asked.

"Sure thing!"

Bacon sizzled in the kitchen while in the bathroom; I washed up and put my clothes on. I was still quite proud of myself, and contemplated my next daring feat. By the time I finished getting dressed, my plate was prepared — bacon, eggs, rice and biscuits. Just like the coffee, he didn't want his biscuits any darker than his skin. He wasn't color struck; he just liked his things the way he liked them.

Because he was the most wonderful daddy on earth, he allowed me to do my own hair that day. So, I grabbed the comb and the ever-famous Royal Crown hair dressing and fixed a six-year-old's version of two ponytails. It had ribbons and a couple of globs of hair grease in the part down the center of my scalp. (That's how Mama did it.) My bangs didn't act right, so I laid them down with Royal Crown, too. I shined like new money!

When I came back into the kitchen to show how pretty I looked, Daddy fell for it again. "You sho' are sharp, Kiddo." I just smiled right back at him, and started to blush as he said, "And look at your hair! It is *so* pretty!" I batted my eyelashes at him as if to say, "Ain't I'm beautiful?"

"Guess what?" he asked while washing a plate.

"What?"

"I'm going to put on my jeans and boots, too. I'll find a blue shirt to wear, and we'll be dressed alike."

That sounded like a wonderful idea to me. This day was off to a great start. No school, a cup of coffee with my Daddy, breakfast *and* he let me do my own hair *and* we'd be dressed alike.

We finished putting away our dishes, turned out the lights and grabbed our matching pleather jackets as we headed out the door for the big city. We were on the outskirts of town when he remembered he hadn't called Mama. He pulled into a gas station to call her. Remember this was 1973, BC...before cell phones. At that time, the only black person in Athens who had a "car phone," as it was called then, was our cousin, Royall Tucker, who owned the funeral home. (And the only person to call on that phone was death.)

Athens had only one radio station, KBUD. That's what we listened to, even though we both detested country music. But unless the weather was great and you had been really good, by chance you might get KKDA from Dallas. Not on this day, though. The sky was overcast, so we didn't stand a chance. But Daddy kept his eight-track tape case in the truck, so we could jam. (There still aren't too many Marvin Gaye songs that I don't know the words to, thanks to my Daddy.)

Daddy opened the truck door, and stepped out to call Mama. As he dialed the number and inserted his dime into the payphone to let Mama know we were on our way, I nearly burst from the excitement of going to Dallas, and from the amusement of how stupid my parents were.

As Daddy finished the phone call, the disc jockey chimed in, "After this station break, we'll give you the school lunch menus for area schools today." Yikes! I turned the radio off so quickly, I nearly yanked the knob out of the dashboard, but just in time.

He got in and cranked the truck and asked, "Didn't I have the radio on?"

"Yes Sir, you did, but I didn't like the song that played so I turned it off."

He laughed, "I don't like that mess either, Baby. Let's see if we can find some news." Reaching past me, he turned KBUD back on. I held my breath, just as the announcer said, "That's it for hot lunch today." I hoped Daddy was thinking about anything else other than lunch menus and school. It was Friday, so I already knew what every child in Athens was having for lunch — hamburgers. Apparently, he knew, too, or perhaps he didn't pay close attention, because he never commented on it.

We were almost to Eustace, when Daddy looked in his rearview mirror and said, "This looks like your Mama behind us. Where is this girl flying to? She's driving like she's lost her mind."

Sure enough, Mama's car weaved in and out of traffic with flashing headlights. Daddy carefully pulled over to see what was wrong. I was certain that she must have forgotten to get some money from him or something. Never did I think my story was about to unravel.

In her nurse's uniform and starched hat, and walking just like Sophia from *The Color Purple,* she marched up to the truck. Before Daddy could roll the window down good, she leaned across his chest and spoke directly to me.

"Patrice, who told you there was no school today?"

I couldn't say a word.

How could she know? I hadn't told anybody about my plan.

Mama said, "I was in the nurse's station, when the man on the radio called out the school lunch menus. Do you know what every other kid in Athens is doing today? They are in school! "

Not a word from me.

"I called the school, and they told me school is in session today. And you are on your way to join them right now! Come on! Get out!"

Busted!

My eyes filled with tears as I sat there, saying nothing. Not only had I forgotten that she listened to KBUD at work. I also forgot that her baby brother (my uncle) was my P.E. teacher at South Athens Elementary. Nor did it dawn on me that she knew how to use a telephone, and would possibly call to verify my story.

"Baby, I'll take her back to school. You just go back to work. I'll take care of this," Daddy said calmly.

Thank God she agreed. That was the closest I had ever come to getting a whipping in my entire six-year-old life. I knew then that I'd never skip school again. She'd kill me.

The ten miles back to Athens was the longest ride I have ever taken. I didn't say anything because I didn't want Daddy to be mad at me. I cared what Mama thought, but I couldn't imagine what it would be like for my best friend to be mad at me.

As we turned into the school parking lot, Daddy asked, "Why did you do this?"

I shrugged my shoulders, "I 'on't know."

Tears no longer dropped, but cascaded down my chubby cheeks. "I just wanted to go with you."

He leaned over and hugged me and said, "Sport, you don't ever have to lie to me in order to get to do something or go somewhere with me. Just ask."

His voice trembled, and as I looked up at him, for the first time in my life, I saw my daddy cry. He wasn't ashamed, nor did he try to hide it from me because as he wiped away his tears, he did the same for mine. "You can go with me whenever I go, wherever I go, just be good."

I asked, "Even to the Flats?" (That's where he would go to shoot craps when he had a little spare change he'd like to get rid of.)

He answered, "Anywhere except the Flats."

That was good enough for me. We walked into the office, holding hands and he signed me in, kissed me and said the usual, "Make me proud."

Over the next four years, my daddy and I would take trips, just for the sake of going somewhere together. We traveled to Mississippi, Arkansas, Louisiana, California, Michigan, and yes, we even drove to Canada.

Five years later, Daddy took a trip without me, but I remember his promise. "You can go with me wherever I go, just be good." He's in heaven now, so I'm doing my best to "be good" so I can go.

***

I'd like to believe I had some pretty good friends growing up. I'm not 100% sure that I was really well liked, more than I was tolerated. Nonetheless, I survived the dog days of junior high with about four of us who were pretty tight. We spent a lot of time together — Mena, Tracy, Lana and me. During that time in our lives we were close enough to be sisters, and for the most part, we shared a good understanding of each other. We even coined our own slogan and put it on a t-shirt. LYLAS... Love Ya Like A Sister.

Mena and I were probably the closest. Our birthdates are two weeks apart. I was born on Janet Jackson's birthday, and she was born on Prince's birthday. During the days of big hair and lots of lace, it was pretty neat for best friends to have celebrity birthdates. Because her mom owned a beauty shop two doors down from my house, I had the chance to hang out with her more than I did the others.

She was the youngest of the group, and I think the prettiest. No, she was definitely the *fine* one. The Native American heritage in her family was evident in her smooth, reddish-brown skin, and beautiful straight hair. By the rest of the world's standards, one may have said she was rotund or heavy set, but she always concluded, "I'm fine; it's the rest of y'all who need to eat." When asked if she ever considered dieting, she would reply, "It's taken me all my life to get this fine, you think I'm gone ruin it with some diet? You crazy!" By far, she was the funniest one of all of us. Unable to make it anywhere on time, she was always the center of our jokes about being slow. Though her mom and dad were divorced, she chose to live with her father, who was equally as much fun as she was.

Tracy was an only child and grew up with the best of everything. She always had the newest shoes, clothes, stereo system, and music. Her house was always the meeting place, and she lived on "the circle," where just about every black teacher in Athens lived. Her mom was a teacher. Tracy was a cheerleader and classical pianist. She would practice for an hour each day, while Mena and I looked on. (I, too, took piano lessons, and let's just say... maybe my parents should have spent that money some other way.)

While we were in the seventh grade, Tracy's mom died. As a result, Tracy was changed forever. None of us could imagine her pain, but we tried to remind her that we were still her sisters. I was a willing a participant when we (approximately 20 junior high girls) decided to skip our lunch and cut afternoon classes to walk to the florist to buy flowers for her. (I don't think anybody's mother knew what we did, until now.) We only wanted to remind her of the words Sisters Sledge had written the year prior, "We Are Family!"

Lana, the independent rebel of the group, marched to the beat of her own drummer, and didn't answer to anybody. Smart and quite clever, if she didn't like the drummer's beat, she'd tell him to change it. If he didn't, she'd change him. Case closed. She's the one, who when her intellectual plate had overflowed with our English lesson, asked Mrs. Curington, "So, what's the point?" Lana was the only one who could say something like that and make the whole class, including the teacher, laugh. She kept us updated and laughing about "the news we could use." Lana would be the last one we expected to end up married to a minister.

Back to this t-shirt thing. When I was growing up, everybody had t-shirts with clever sayings on them. You were especially cool in junior high if you put the name of a song on your t-shirt. I actually had my mother buy a shirt for me that read, "Upside Down & Round and Round." How goofy was that? Remember the Diana Ross song? But wait, there's more. I had the letters put on, upside down, with round and round circling it!

Our LYLAS Sisterhood days were a blast. Those memories still bring a sentimental grin to my face. A typical Saturday afternoon for us would be to meet at one person's house, usually Tracy's, to watch Soul Train, after Fat Albert went off. (Rudy was so cute. I loved his boots.) I always wanted to find out what it took to be on Soul Train. I knew if they'd just let me, I could do the scramble board in plenty of time, in order to wave to all of my family back in Athens. But as life would have it, I never made it to the show. If I had made it, chances are, I would have been the first person to misspell Dr. Martin L. King, and bring disgrace on my family and black people everywhere. But at least I would have been on television.

After watching Soul Train, we would then prepare for our *walk* downtown to buy something to wear to the junior college football game happening later that night, and then *walk* to a favorite restaurant to have lunch. Then we'd *walk* home, all excited about what we had bought. We would get back to the house and pull out our outfits, remarking to each other just how sharp we would be. We would do each other's hair and get dressed. We'd take a quick "wash off," but never a bath. That would take too long. But we were the sharpest group in town. It was junior high school fun. We were only twelve years old, but we walked everywhere, and had a great time doing it.

{Please press PAUSE} This brings me to the first of many jewels of reflection you will unearth, while sitting on the front porch with me.{Press PLAY}

When water was free, your twelve-year-old daughters could spend the day walking with friends or shopping without the worry of being abducted (or arrested).

I always did well in school. I graduated in the top 20 percent of my class of 167 students. In fact, I probably could have been an honor graduate, but was not compelled to overexert my brain.

I was never the homecoming queen type, but I was always one of the few "tokens" on the committees at school. Yes, we had token blacks in "Big A" and it wasn't a bad thing, then. That's just how it was. I should know because I was one. We would have representation in the right places, but it wasn't always equal.

For instance, we would have school dances and the disc jockey would play soul music, but the two songs he would play would be heard at about 11:45 pm, when the dance was over at midnight. We paid our $3.00, just like the others. So, yes, I learned all the words to Bon Jovi, Eddie Van Halen, and Kenny Rogers, and danced "The Cotton Eyed Joe" not by choice. If we, the black kids, wanted to have something to do after the games, we went to the dances and danced to their music until our two songs were played. It didn't bother us then, and helped to prepare me for a life that will *never* treat *everyone* equally. That's not necessarily a bad thing. I learned at an early age, how to deal with issues such as these, so by the time I made it to Corporate America, I was already prepared. It was no great shock to me that we, as a people, still pay our dues, but are often still the last to dance.

My circle and I didn't miss a football game, basketball game, prom, bonfire, homecoming game or anything else significant. We were there! Homecoming was probably the most fun we would have during the first semester. It became the "best excuse to go shopping" for the big dance after the game. The whole week of the homecoming game was filled with activities: the parade, the bonfire, and midnight pep rallies. The air was thick with excitement. Even the students who rarely participated in school activities showed more enthusiasm during homecoming week. The teachers also seemed to find as much enjoyment as the students. Girls like me and my crew, "The Weekend Girls," with no boyfriends could only imagine what it was like for a boy to buy a mum for them. (This is probably one of the few times Mama wished that I did have a boyfriend, so she wouldn't have to pay for yet *another* mum.) However, because I was single every year for homecoming, I'd just randomly select somebody from the football team whose jersey number would look good on my mum. Then I'd have it put it on there…without his permission. Who cared? It was my mum and my mama's money.

When water was free, a homecoming mum was a simple flower, with a few ribbons and maybe a bell, or some other trinket!

Today's mums should be outlawed, or be required to meet certain requirements by the Department of Defense or the Bureau of Alcohol, Tobacco and Firearms. Last year, as I dropped off my niece at her senior homecoming game, one of the homecoming queen nominees arrived, just as I pulled out of the parking lot. I was amazed at what I was thought was a mum, but more closely resembled a floral covered breast plate, which flapped over her shoulder to make a white floral backpack, as well. Not only did it appear that she must have had to slide into the protective armor, as a knight would, but also it came equipped with battery-operated Christmas lights. (Dear God, I prayed for a night free of lightning.)

The entire outfit looked heavy enough to cause back problems. Just looking at all of the flowers made me want to sneeze. The only thing this little "knightette" didn't have was a helmet. Then again, if she was named the winner, she'd get a crown, so go figure that one out. I thought to myself, *There's no way such a petite little frame could balance that curtain and a crown. Poor thing. Her mother should be ashamed.*

The month was October, but I could have sworn I was looking at Bing Crosby's rendition of "White Christmas." She and her entire outfit matched to a tee. Everything was white...the mum, the streamers blowing in the evening breeze, and the lights. Who was she, the homecoming queen or the Christmas queen? Was this homecoming or the Christmas parade? Where were her eight tiny reindeer?

I felt like stopping my car to yell out of the window, "People Please!!! This frightens me!!!" I wanted to ask her mother, "Exactly what in the world was on your mind when you let her order this mess? But, I realized that probably was none of my business, and I should continue driving out of the parking lot, before the Christmas parade began.

As I drove off, I realized my oldest daughter was only ten years old then, which meant we would have four years until high school. Since the stock market crash after 9/11, my 401k has not performed very well. I just hope it rebounds in time for me to start purchasing chrysanthemum gardens, so my Jordie will have a homecoming mum, even if I have to grow it and make it myself. If that's not possible, maybe I can get a second job to afford one. By then, the homecoming mum attire will be an entire dress made of mums, streamers and lights, with the matching floral helmet and a sword, instead of a scepter and gloves. Yikes!

I'll never forget homecoming night during my senior year. You'll soon see why.

My posse, LYLAS had outgrown the childish moniker, and had matured to "The Weekend Girls". As I made the familiar turn down the dark and winding road to the "Dad's Club Park," in Malakoff, the girls and I were already pumped for the party. This Friday night would be no different. The four of us had donated the customary $2.00 per person for gasoline for my car, for the weekend, which meant we collectively still had about $72.00 to last us through Sunday. We all had on our neon sweatshirts, signature gold chains dangling heavily from our necks. Our Nikes were new and the Levi 501 jeans were, too. The three-dollar admission was all you needed to dance until two o'clock in the morning, if your parents allowed you to stay out that long. The week prior, I learned the hard way that my mama didn't play that.

It was really a *simple* mistake. See, it was the weekend that daylight savings time was changed back to standard time. Mama told me to be home by 1 a.m. Around our house, we had always set our clocks back before going to bed. Well, in my seventeen-year-old mind, she was already asleep, and she didn't tell me which one o'clock she meant. (I guess I had forgotten about the last time I thought she was stupid.) It was when she pulled up at the party, in our Chevrolet station wagon, that I quickly realized which one she had spoken of. She methodically stepped out of the car to make certain that I knew it was her. As she made her way through the clearing being made by my friends, the crowds separated, reminding me of the scene from the Ten Commandments when Moses parted the Red Sea. (And I was scared as Pharoah's soldiers. I knew I was dead.) I think everybody was equally as scared for me as I was. She cleared her throat and said, "Uh, excuse me, Patrice; are you planning on coming back to *my* house to sleep tonight?"

"Yes ma'am, I'm coming," I sheepishly answered, while digging around in my pockets for my car keys.

"Well, if that's the case, *your car* better beat *my car* back to the house, or you won't get in," she exclaimed sharply with her parenthood in full bloom.

I knew she meant business, so I got to it. It only took me about thirty seconds to round everyone up to get home before her. I made it. By the time she made it home, I had dropped Mena off at home and was undressed and in bed. I lay there silently expecting the worse. I think she made a couple of extra blocks so she wouldn't have to kill me; I still thank her for it.

Instead of knocking my teeth out, she made me get out of bed, and she got on her fifty-six year old knees and prayed. "God, please watch over this fool. I've given her more than any seventeen year old in Athens has, and she doesn't appreciate it. I pay her car note, and insurance, and *all* I ask her to do is to come home on time. Apparently, God, she can't tell time, anymore. I don't know what to do, but I'm doing my best for her. So, just protect her when she's not being obedient to her only parent. Amen."

Why didn't she just beat me? By the time she finished praying, I was reduced to sobs and tears. I couldn't even apologize. I felt terrible and didn't sleep well that night. I tip-toed around her for a few days, making certain not to mention anything that may remotely remind her of that night. Homecoming was only a few days away, and I couldn't mess up. When I found the guts to ask to go out again the next weekend, she allowed me to go, but the girls and I fully understood, "We are outta here at 12:45 a.m."

As I parked the car, I looked into my rearview mirror and noticed an unfamiliar, but obviously new Toyota Supra immediately behind me. The car's bass boomed out the sounds of Whodini's "Five Minutes of Funk." We bounced as Jalil rapped, "Pull your bottom off the tree stump, ladies lookin' pretty from city to city, now I'm getting down to the nitty gritty." By that time, we didn't need to pay the admission; the party had started in the parking lot, right next to my dusty '82 Thunderbird.

When the door to the unknown vehicle opened, the girls and I lost our rhythmic bounce, as the occupants of the vehicle emerged. It was them — the heffas we couldn't stand. And now one of them had a new car? We, in an unrehearsed synchronized chord, all said together, "Oh Hell No!" The silent alarm was sounded. We knew that tonight, we'd have to prove "The Weekend Girls" were still the hottest, hippest, flyest girls at the party, even though we didn't have the newest ride.

This would be the night that we didn't care about the $25 hairdos we had just paid for. We were going to sweat those hairstyles out, while out dancing *them*. Any chants to ring out during the party would be started and ended by *The Girls*. "If ya don't wanna party, then you should go home, getcha hat, getcha coat, getcha sh*t, and get gone." We drew the line in the sand, and maintained our position. Was it jealousy? Maybe. Aww naw, we were just protecting our reps. (Reputations....come on now, I know you remember those days.) Now please understand, we were better than no one; but they definitely were no better than us. Truth is these girls were just as pretty as we were, just as intelligent as we were, and probably more disciplined as any of my crew, but we could have never admitted that.

The legal capacity of the three hundred square foot room was around fifty people; however, when AJ the DJ pumped up the volume, no less than two hundred people crowded into the dank, wooden-floored clubhouse. The aluminum foil on the windows rattled as AJ made his rounds through the crowds. "AJ will Rock U Ova," he bellowed through the cordless mike, as his back up DJ continued mixing and scratching... "DJ please pick up your phone, I'm on the request line..."

You knew you were *the girl* if AJ sent a shout out to you. That night, he knew what was up with us and them, and the first one to get the shout out would win.

When George Clinton's "Atomic Dog" came on, it didn't matter who you danced with, you just needed to find somebody and stake your claim on the dance floor. There wasn't much room to begin with, but you had to find a spot.

If you couldn't fit onto the dance floor, you had to climb up on a speaker or dance on a table or something. (No, not like that... in a clean, 1984 way.) Even those people outside who couldn't make it inside would dance on the front porch. AJ would mix the song for no less than twenty minutes and we all danced until it went off.

I don't know if there were any bona fide Omega brothers actually there, but the joint sounded just like "The Dawg Pound." RROOOOOFFF! Even the girls barked. The weakening floor buckled beneath us, as everybody stomped until they were all barked out. I often worried how many more parties that place could take at the rate we were going. But twenty years later, it is still in tact.

Kids today don't know how to party like we did. Every weekend there were at least two hundred people together, but no guns or knives. If a fight broke out, it was just a chance to break away from the party for a breath of fresh air. The fighters fought to the finish, dusted themselves off and returned to the party. Chances are, if "Atomic Dog" came on, the fight would end like this, "Negro, you better be glad my song is on, or I'd beat your butt," as the crowds made a beeline for the clubhouse.

Of course, there was alcohol, but *The Weekend Girls* didn't drink that junk. And we certainly didn't do drugs or associate with those who did, to our knowledge.

As the tempo and temperature of the party intensified, and the body heat elevated from two hundred black folk, fifty of whom found it impossible to part ways with the Jeri Curl, which added to the heat, it didn't take long for us to get hot and thirsty. Nobody, but nobody went home looking or smelling as good as they did when they came. It just couldn't happen. Man! It was hot.

Mena, who despite her body blessing, danced better than ninety percent of the people there. She and I were dancing near each other. In the midst of doing the Weekend Girls version of "The Prep," I motioned for her to meet me outside for a breather. I made my way to the door, with my hair stuck to my sweaty face, when she reminded me, "Tracy forgot to buy the sodas when we stopped to get gas, and there ain't nothing but beer inside. Girl, ain't no water no where, but in the bathroom sink." We had a decision to make. "Whatchu think?

"I'on't know, girl."

Did we drink water from the sink in the women's bathroom, or did we drink a beer? Contemplating our choices, reputations and values, we headed back inside.

Mena and I weaved through the crowds standing shoulder-to-shoulder, shoulder-to-chin and shoulder-to-breast, and headed to the back of the room, near the bathrooms. She opened the door to the refrigerator and grabbed the first beer within sight, and handed it to me, with a huge smile on her face. We struggled together to unscrew the top. AJ was across the room, but noticed our struggle and watched practically in tears as he laughed because the biggest squares in Athens had a beer. He headed our way, as we embarked on our maiden voyage toward becoming beer drinkers. He graciously twisted the top off for us, and handed it back to us, laughing so hard, he couldn't say anything. He just turned and walked away. That's all right. We didn't care. It was hot, and Mena and I chugged that beer, just like it was free water. It was almost like we knew what we were doing. All I remember is it was cold and tasted like bad breath with ginger ale. Maybe that's why at thirty-seven, I still don't like the stuff.

I don't remember if we won the homecoming game or not, but what I do remember is that we did get the first shout out at the party. And all of it came as a result of my homegirl and me drinking our first beer. I also recall that I made it home on time.

It has been said that a woman's best friends know enough about her to put her away. That's definitely true for us. As children, we enjoyed a great friendship, building our arsenal of bribes on each other. Although as we grew older and grew apart, there is still love between us, but words spoken and deeds done sometimes alter our perspectives of those closest to us. I love them no less, but have found my true joy is in my family. I am sure they have found the same.

***

During my senior year we had a black quarterback, which resulted in our school having the first winning football season (6-4) in years. So, we made the best of it. It was a great year at Athens High, home of the fighting Hornets.

"On, on you hornets, fight to the end"

"On, on you hornets, victory you'll win"

"On, on you hornets, into the fray"

"For your name will live on, after this day!"

I was in the pep squad and then in the marching band. There has never been an athletic bone (muscle, tissue, cell, molecule, mitochondria, nucleus, endoplasmic reticulum...) in my body. I never wanted to play sports, but enjoyed watching them. Basketball was my favorite.

I never ran and only ventured outside when I was really, really bored. I could not, and still can't, run unless there's a grasshopper or a cat within reasonable distance. In which case, I could probably outrun Marion Jones, the Olympic sprinter.

It's also notable that in a town as small as Athens, and as top heavy in the Caucasian demographic, our high school band director was black. Despite what you may think, we marched with military precision every Friday night. Shined white shoes, polished brass, starched uniforms and white plumes were trademarks of the Pride of the Hornets Marching Band. If you didn't have enough elbow grease (energy) for polishing buttons, shoes and breast plates, you didn't march, no matter how well you played, or who your daddy was.

My friend Tracy and I both played bass clarinet and beamed with pride when we performed our UIL marching contest drill. When the band executed the marching X maneuver, we were the two people in the center of the X. *We* were the ones in the center of the show. Man, we hoped that our director would just lose his mind, and let us get downright funky, like Grambling or Prairie View A&M, just *one* time. But thank God he was smarter than us. The first time he would have ever allowed that, we would have been looking for a new drill and he would have been looking for a new job! It's good to know that adults really did know what was best for us, both then and now. He's retiring this year from the district, but as the assistant superintendent in the district. Go on then! I'm proud to have been one of his band brats.

***

You have to understand, Athens, TX is 10,197 people strong. and the demographics in 1985, when I graduated, did not really reflect an ethnic diversity. It's my hometown, and I love it dearly. However, I am reminded of an incident that year, when a good friend (black male) went to the local country club as a guest of another friend (white female) to play tennis. The president of the school board made him leave. That never sat well with me. Nor did the way white teens were permitted to congregate in the parking lot of a grocery store downtown. When black kids did similarly at a school "across the tracks," police demanded that the north side crowds disperse. I'm still not quite certain on the difference between the two. Both groups were in violation of loitering ordinances, but only one group was demanded to leave. Neither was unruly, and neither possessed alcohol nor drugs. Was this separate but equal treatment? The jury is still out. So, while I love my hometown, it hasn't always shared the love or embraced all of the family the way it should. Things are changing for the better, however. Athens has yet to crown its first black Miss Athens; but I was the second runner-up in *Miss Black Henderson County, 1985*. Although the tracks still separate north and south Athens, former north-side residents now live in Bel-Air.

My mother still lives there, and I love going home because it's only an hour away, and I can still get there in time for dinner. (Which I often do, after working a full day.) Even with the controversial racial relations I mentioned, it never affected our household. My mama wouldn't stand for it.

Physically, I was always a skinny little girl. I'm still rather small, thirty something years later. The sandy brown thick hair that I have is courtesy of my paternal grandmother, whose hair was so big, it was almost intimidating. So, not only did I inherit her first name, she also gave me this hair, which resembles chocolate cotton candy. It's coarse and thick and the devil to manage when it gets wet. Before the days when Mama trusted a lye permanent for my hair, I spent my share of Saturday mornings straddled across a stool with a pillow on it, while she pressed my hair. Two hours of sizzling, frying hair, while Mama and Royal Crown declared war on my naps. That's why when I finally got a perm, I promised God if he *ever* delivered me from that can of Royal Crown, I'd never use it again. (Now she's got my kids hooked on it.)

When the humidity is high, I can forget about the *bouncy and managed* Claire Huxtable look. No way. Humid days call for the big guns. Water, brush and gel, not just any gel, but Dippity-Do, and Aqua Net and Royal Crown to give it a shine. (Remember them?) Neither of the first two products was made with black folk in mind, but they really worked well together with the Royal Crown to tame the chocolate cotton candy and hold it in place.

On high humidity days, I still wet a brush thoroughly to slick my hair back into a ponytail. I apply a generous glob of gel to my hands to smooth it out, (just like I did when I was six) and a couple of sprays of Aqua Net to hold the look, and a little Royal Crown to make it shine. I'll then put on red lipstick, tint my eyebrows a little darker than normal, and spend the day as a Texas version of Sade, the sultry R&B diva. She and I share the same honey cream skin tone and a similar forehead size. (Don't say a word.)

I have my mother's light brownish-green eyes and fair skin, although I look more like my father's people. However, when I'm with my mother's family, they say I look just like her. So, who really knows? Maybe Mama and Daddy looked alike?

A guy I once dated introduced me to his family, and his uncle smiled and said I resembled a "nappy-headed Puerto Rican." Others who see me assume that I am a Creole Louisiana babe. Nope. That's not me, either. Many try to figure out if I'm bi-racial.

When water was free, we called that, "mixed." But now that would sound like a salad, rather than a racial ethnicity.

But no, I am black! My mama and daddy and their parents before them were black, so that makes me black. Anyway, after digging around anyone's family tree, not just ours, time will usually reveal something a little different than what they are now.

I'm not yet African American because I have not yet been to Africa. And much to the dismay of many of my soul brothers and sisters, I have no desire to go. This makes me no less black than the brothers and sisters of Africa who have no desire to visit the USA. This is where I was born, and this is where I hope to die. I love the good old U S of A and her Caribbean islands. Deal with it.

When water was free, it was okay to be black, but now we are African American. Go figure.

Chapter

2 "The Tribe of Jordan"

How did you get here? Glad you asked! I am the great granddaughter of a white slave owner who raped his teenaged Negro slave. When she later revealed to him that she was pregnant from his brutal attack, he took a rifle and went for a one-way walk in the cemetery. He never came back. He killed himself in shame.

From that disgraceful act of cowardice sprang generations of great pride. My maternal grandfather, Ruben Jordan, would grow up and leave his hometown, and move north to Athens, and marry the most beautiful woman in Athens, my grandmother, Ruth Massey. He would become a highly regarded chef in Athens, and the even higher respected father of eight children. He was a well-dressed, fair skinned man of few words because he stuttered. But he loved his Ruthie and lovingly called her "Nigger," due to the richness of her sun-kissed skin.

Because of his well-respected position with the good white folk downtown, he was able to provide a standard of living for his family that could be matched by only a few. He purchased a new car every other year for his family. Also, Paw-Paw Jordan was one of the few people in Athens to have a telephone in the late 1930s. My grandparents were the only blacks at that time in the small bustling city to afford such a luxury. They would accept telephone calls for all of the blacks in Athens, and instruct their children to "run this message *'cross town'*." But just for the record, lest I lead you to believe that they were anything more than they were; my Granny and Paw-Paw were not too good to pick cotton. And they did so whenever there was a need to make ends meet.

Paw-Paw Jordan was a Baptist; Granny was from the Church of the Living God, PGT. They worshipped at separate locations for a few years until Paw-Paw spoke those famous words recorded by Luke the physician. In my mind's ear, I can hear him as he struggled to get his tongue and brain to work as a team. He stood his ground, while speaking to my granny and said:

"Ninnigger, The word seh (says) aaa house di-di-di-divided 'ginst itssssself, won't st-st-st-stand." (Luke 11:17c)

"Y-y-you comin' to chutch wit me."

From that point, "The Tribe of Jordan" became one family of one faith, in one God, worshiping at Mount Providence Baptist Church, until about the late 1980s. We have since scattered again, and now we can be found in every major organized denomination today.

My mother, Emmaline Jordan Kissentaner was the "baby girl," and she brought the sunshine into her daddy's day. Before becoming old enough to cook, Paw-Paw took her under his culinary wing and taught her a "cooking sauce" recipe for basting barbecue. It still remains a family secret today. He only shared it with his baby girl. She has shared the recipe with one nephew, and he is now responsible for where it goes. (However, I didn't wait for her to bequeath it to me. I figured it out for myself, and there is no beer in the recipe!) The meat is so flavorful, tender, and moist that you mess it up by putting commercially bottled sauce on it. Let's put it like this, on your way to heaven, ask God to let you swing through Athens, Texas to sample my mama's barbecue. (The only natural thing would be to go to heaven after tasting it.) I am honored to know that the greatest cook who ever lived gave birth to me.

Recently, I took a poll of others who have sampled some of her recipes to see what they thought was the best dish she's ever prepared. Those involved in the conversation mentioned things I hadn't even thought of and many that I had, including baked ham, potato salad, dressing, barbecued ribs, fried catfish, cream peas, macaroni and cheese, sweet potato pies, homemade candy, and fresh apple cake. That went on for about one minute non-stop. It makes me hungry, just thinking about it.

So, you see, it is proven that I come from a long line of skilled craftsmen (women) who can "hold their own" in the kitchen. This just confirms that I come from cooking royalty. Paw-Paw was the king; Mama is the princess; and that makes me the "Lady". I love to cook, but I can't help it; it's in my genes.

Over the years, our family would eventually establish my mother's role as the matriarch of the modern day "Tribe of

Jordan." My mother is seventy-five years old and simply radiant. She has aged with timeless grace, and not one wrinkle is found on her smooth caramel-colored skin. (It's too full. Her cheeks seem to glow when she smiles.) Much like those long, silky black strands of hair that faded and now glisten silvery platinum, her hearing is fading, but she reminds us, "I hear what I want to hear. If my grandchildren need me, I can hear them just fine. But if it's just some mess going on, I can't hear it, and I don't know if I really want to. Besides, at seventy-five years old, I've heard enough stuff to last me a lifetime." Her hearing aid is still in its box in her purse, and she says it works wonderfully, in there.

That's the kind of wit that has sustained this pillar of strength and beauty all of her life. She's unequivocally honest; if you don't want the truth, don't ask her. She's frank and sometimes void of tact. But she only means it for your well being. Even at seventy-five, she remains independent and does not care for us "looking after" her. She drives herself wherever she wants to go, and is afraid of nothing and no one. Her .38 revolver rests comfortably beside her bed, next to her Bible opened to Psalm 91. Needless to say, she sleeps well at night.

Just this year, the former first lady, Barbara Bush, wrote a book and was featured on an evening television show. As she spoke about her years at the White House, and life since then, I was impressed with her account of day-to-day life in the "Papa George Bush" White House. It was interesting to me that though she is well respected, she is stern, but funny. Those same characteristics remind me so very much of my mother. I found it remarkable that both recognize that grandchildren are much more fun than children. But when I thought about their differences, I got an even greater laugh.

Aside from one being black and the other white, one is a democrat, the other is in denial. Think about this:

BB- Lived at 1600 Pennsylvania Avenue, the most prestigious address in the U.S., only for four years.

EJK- For forty-eight years has lived at 210 Massey, a street named for her great grandfather, and through her tax dollars, she helped to pay for Barbara Bush to live in Washington.

BB- Gave birth to a son, who was not very smart, acquired a drinking problem, but who would become the forty-sixth governor of Texas, and forty-third president of the United States.

EJK- Grandmother of a grandson (Andy) who is really quite smart, hasn't quite learned how to drink, but grew up to protect and serve Barbara Bush's not so smart son.

BB- In order to visit Barbara Bush, a federal security clearance is required, and the approval of the Secret Service.

EJK- In order to visit Emmaline, just drive down Massey Street, she's usually sitting on the porch. But you may have to get past, Jordan, Jamie, Rudy, Tiffany April, Ashley, AJ, Kendrick, Nikki, Chris, De, Aliyah, Jay and Tray — the executive board and fan club. The board of directors is made up of her grandchildren, great grandchildren and great-great grandchildren. Trust me; it may be easier to get past the U.S. Secret Service, than to tackle this bunch.

BB- It is an honor to be invited to dine with Barbara Bush.

EJK- It is an honor to get to sample anything she cooks.

-Thousands of visitors have gone to the White House

Not one visitor has been to 210 Massey Street; once you go there, you are always at home.

Barbara Bush's official title was First Lady of the United States of America

EJK-Emmaline's impressive titles are too many to name, but some of the most important ones are "Mama," "Maw-Maw," "Big Mama" and "Queen of the Tribe called Jordan."

Even without her charming conversation or delectable dining table, Mama's front yard is a comforting floral experience all its own. Her (wo)manicured lawn is dutifully groomed and proves that she not only has a green thumb, but also a red one, yellow, pink and orange, and on and on. In the spring, vibrant plant life radiates all around her. It's as though in late March, like the conductor of an orchestra, she steps onto the front porch and calls the roll. From their seasonal sleep beneath their earthly beds, each flower drowsily answers "Here, Ma'am." Within the coming days, they wake up, stand up, and tune up their floral vocal chords with a song of life and love, written especially for her. The front yard sings in harmony with energetic color; a rhapsody of roses in red, a chorus of camellias in coral, with a tempo of tulips in tangerine. And there she is, Naomi Emmaline Jordan-Kissentaner, "The Em," standing barely five feet tall, conducting the symphony.

The Easter lilies stand alone in their own sanctuary of the yard. Daffodils dance in the cool breeze, as the pollen from neighboring cottonwood trees engage the allergic in their own sonata of sneezes. The rose bushes are named for each of her children and are the most highly regarded flowers in her own Garden of Eden. Within the tranquility and beauty of this quaint corner of her yard lies an invisible perimeter of the danger zone, whose borders are only known to the curator of these private grounds. For one's own safety, one should not take a shortcut by walking through *these* flower beds, at the risk of losing an appendage. These blossoms are her perennial friends, which she expects to see year after year, as she tends to their every need year round.

"Ain't nobody gon' walk on my children and they sho' ain't gon' walk on my flowers...and I mean that!"

Even as her garden harmonizes a concerto of vivid colors, she takes time to prune the flowers, to cut them back and share their beauty with others. She gives them to people in the hospital, or nursing homes, for birthdays, or just because. It doesn't matter to her. "Flowers are for sharing," she concedes.

As a child, I didn't understand why she would cut her pretty flowers, just to give them away. She'd reply, "Baby, it's just a flower. When I cut them back, another one'll grow in its place and will be prettier than this one. It's just waiting for a chance to bloom. Just wait and see."

I still didn't understand until a similar pruning happened to me later in life. Now, I understand just how smart my mama is.

Recently at Mama's seventy-fifth birthday party, while my brother Andy spoke, he provoked our thoughts with the following:

He said, "We grew up poor, but never knew it. That's how you know you've been blessed."

That's so true because Mama worked to take care of us. We had all the designer jeans during the 80s. We all got cars while we were in high school, and she kept a new car, as well. Those who don't know God don't understand how we maintained. However, we know fully well that by the grace of God we were blessed — over and over and over again. We weren't lucky; we were blessed. The difference between being lucky and being blessed is in whom you place your trust. Those who believe in people, lottery numbers and four-leafed clovers tend to get lucky. But those who trust God are blessed. It's just that simple. I haven't found lucky rabbits feet, four leaf clovers or genies in a bottle in the Bible, but I am well aware of the accounts of having great faith. Rewards for faithfulness has been proven true for me more times that I can count. But this ain't regular Sunday school; this is just some sweet front-porch theology.

Mama, a licensed nurse for decades, took pride in wearing her white uniform, white hose, white shoes, and starched white nurse's cap. She becomes offended now, when she sees nurses wearing brightly colored scrubs and sneakers to work. "It's just not professional," she comments every time we visit the hospital.

She worked for doctors in the hospitals delivering babies, in surgery, in nursing homes, and before retiring she did private health care. People still recognize her in town, and come up to reintroduce her to a now grown adult, who she assisted with delivering, thirty or forty years ago. She smiles sweetly, but doesn't remember half of them. I'll ask, "Ma, who was that?" She'll laugh and say, "Honey, I only wish I knew!"

During the segregation era of the 1960s, when blacks were hardly welcomed at the local hospital, Mama served as a midwife for those who couldn't afford to give birth there, or were not allowed in the building because of the color of their skin. Our skin was too dark, but our money wasn't green enough. Kinda like in the justice system.

When water was free, justice came with a price tag that most black people couldn't afford. Until O.J. Simpson bought the platinum package, and ultimately his freedom. (By then, water was no longer free, but he was.)

One night after refusing to eat in the "colored section" of the cafeteria, a little room Mama still describes as "the broom closet," she raised quite a stink around the hospital. That night she ate dinner in the area reserved for her white coworkers and subordinates. She wrote a note to her supervisor, detailing what she had done. Fearlessly, she spared no words in confronting the issue. The incident made the local paper, and our own Athenian version of the civil rights struggle began compliments of my dear mother.

This happened before I was born, but she often reminds me of whom all she "let have it" when that happened, and how those who had been unsupportive of her, now seem awkwardly devoted to her because of the invariable stand she took.

The entire episode was not the issue; her problem was that she had worked all day, doing whatever was needed, as her supervisor entrusted the entire floor to her. Mama did the jobs, but the doctors were paid for them. So when a bigoted few refused to let her eat with them, well, quite naturally, she spoke up. They heard and she resigned. As she left, she recalls telling them that she had no desire to work there anymore, as she had accepted a position in a neighboring county as Director of Nurses for a nursing home. And with that she was gone!

I'm glad she did because within the next two years, her cousin would introduce her to the handsome guy who would later become her husband and my father, Leonard Clifton Kissentaner.

***

She never whipped me. Even after the first grade skipped class and the which-one-o'clock-did-you-mean episode, she talked to me. This is many people's assessment of what's wrong with me, but that's *their* opinion. As our conversation continued, she helped me understand my role in our relationship.

When water was free, parents were parents; kids were kids. Today, kids are parents, literally, before the age of eighteen.

She was my mother, I was the kid.

We could talk about anything, but I guess I had too much respect for her because I would have *never* approached the subject of sex with her. I don't care how much she said we could talk about it.

When water was free, children were less likely to discuss sex with their parents, due mainly to that awkward respect we had for them.

It was a sign of the times. Nowadays, parents are more friendly with their children, and less authoritative. Somewhere along the way, we parents didn't read our entire contract thoroughly. We have opted for what is easy, as opposed to what is right. We have skipped the fine print and chosen to save our child's feelings as opposed to disciplining them at the time when they are disobedient.

Not me! I've been a mother for twelve years, and I have yet to promise either of my daughters a spanking. If their actions warrant some correction, I do so, on the spot. Of course, I don't beat them, but I refuse to let the situation carry on, disrupting my day. So, we deal with it. Most of the time, we can talk about it and reach a positive resolution. Other times warrant other actions.

Nothing infuriates me more than hearing a parent say, "When we get home, I'm going to…" or "I'm going to tell your father." Hellooooo? You and the child both know that by the time you get home, you will have forgotten. Chances are, your little angel will do something else even more nerve wracking. And poor old dad won't have a clue about why you, Mom, are so frazzled. Then when he replies, "Why didn't you just spank him?" you'll become angry with Dad for not supporting you. Handle your business when it needs to be handled. Or call me, I'll help you.

Many may ask why I spank my children when my mother did not spank me. Well, here it is. I spank my children because they are around other people's children (not necessarily yours) whose lack of values has unfortunately rubbed off on mine. For instance, the temper tantrums others allow their children to have would never work with me. Day care helped usher this in.

My generation never went to commercialized, franchised day care. No. We were "kept" by home care providers, who did so for little or no money. Mrs. Staples' and Mrs. Rose's pre-school were run by older Christian women who loved children and turned no one away from their homes. They had all the rights and privileges of parents, and could be trusted with anyone's children.

When water was free, pre-school meant your child spent the day under the care of someone who loved them and had time to spend with them.

I had the pleasure of watching our youngest daughter, Jamie, throw her first and only temper tantrum on a hot, summer day while we lived in South Carolina. She had asked to go outside, and I refused to let her go because it was too hot. I told her we would go out later when it cooled off. To that response, she took it upon herself to fall out, right there on my kitchen floor. All two years and twenty-five pounds of her kicked and screamed like a maniac. I happened to have a glass of ice water in my hand while I stood there, in amazement, watching this spectacle of a toddler trauma. At first, she caught me off guard because I had never seen either of my children behave this way. I thought to myself, "This is not my child."

Apparently our oldest daughter, Jordan, who was approximately four at the time, was equally as shocked. She peeked around the kitchen corner, keeping a safe distance between herself and her sister. Jordie needed to see what was wrong with her, too. The look on her face said it all, "Jamie, you have lost your mind!" In that instance, as Jamie started to spin around on the floor like a break dancer, I dashed the entire glass of cold water onto the toddler screaming on the floor.

Within the moment and in the twinkling of an eye, she was changed. She was startled, and immediately hushed. She got up from the floor, drenched, and walked away, looking back every now and then to make sure I wasn't behind her. I didn't follow her. I just stared at her to let her know that yes, I was just as silly as she was. She went to her room, changed her own clothes, and came back downstairs to rejoin her family, with no mention of the recent mind lapse she suffered. I could hear her thinking aloud, "I bet I'll never do that again. That woman is crazy!"

That was 1995, and I'm happy to report that nine years later, we've not seen her flailing on the floor, kicking and screaming since.

Time-out *is for basketball,* when a player is injured. It's not for disciplining children. I'm still looking for the dysfunctional joker who came up with this mess. This suburban faux pas has contributed greatly in the creation today's misfits in society. Has anyone from the country ever used time out? I don't think so. Aw naww, you better get a belt or switch (a small vine like branch from a bush or small tree, for you city folk) and get that matter resolved, right now. Time-out is the biggest *uh-oh* around today. Making little Sean stand in the corner is not going to stop his bad behavior. It only gives that rascal a minute to rest up, refuel his tank, and restart his rampage, firing from all pistons. You can keep sending your children to time-out, and I'll keep correcting mine the way I choose. Let's see whose child ends up in juvenile court first. I bet it won't be mine!

When water was free, disciplining children was an expression of care for the well being of children.

Back then, people were genuinely concerned for each other. If a child misbehaved, he or she could expect to be corrected and, if necessary, chastised (not beaten) by anybody and everybody who knew about their dirty deed. This included, and was not limited to, parents, teachers, neighbors, and relatives. Basically, any adult could discipline any child, regardless of whose they were. I was never spanked, not because I was such a wonderful child, but because Mama said she was too old to chase me around to whip me.

For many reasons, today we can no longer continue with this expression of love and care. The children have not changed, but society has. There are some real losers out there, who prey on hurting children. Then there are those of you parents who don't think your little terror can do any wrong.

You are in denial. They can and they do. I know because mine do. And I did, too.

When water was free, children would never consider mumbling or talking back to an adult, especially if they were within a house shoe's throw of an adult. It had nothing to do with fear, but rather respect for adults.

Now, on the other hand, when we got far enough away from the adults (like a block and a half away) we may have said something.

Today, I see far too many adults entertaining conversations with children, which need not be. If one of my children would ask me "Why?" after I had instructed them to do something, my reply would be "Because I make the rules, buy the clothes, pay the mortgage, book the cruises, pay for modeling classes, buy the track uniforms, pay for the new hairdo, drive the car, go to work every day and I do not report to you." To that end, we would strike up another conversation. But some of you waste valuable time trying to reason with your children. Reason with them for what? A two-year-old doesn't understand reasoning. You are the adult. Act like it. Please be reminded, I am not offering "Parenting 101." This is just frank talk from the front porch, when water was free.

When water was free, parents were parents and kids were kids, end of discussion.

I have a problem with children who are disrespectful and talk back. And those who elect to see exactly how far they can stretch their luck don't fare very well with me. I have zero tolerance for bad kids. Yes, there are such things as bad kids. You know it as well as I do. The ones you see in the grocery story screaming or the ones who fall out on the floor, in an effort to get their way…those are bad kids. And you are a bad parent if you stand there, ignoring them and allowing your children to behave that way. They act that way because you allow them to. So actually, it's the parents who need help, just as much as the children. (If you don't like what you've just read, write your book, but please keep reading this one.)

My children, who know my limits, sometimes forget because they see others getting away with bad behavior with their parents, and they want to see if it'll work on me. Not here. Wrong household. Remember Jamie and the glass of water?

When water was free, crying babies were a sign to the parents that something was wrong.

Today, I think babies simply cry, just to make noise. It couldn't be that the parents are ignoring them, could it? Of course it could be. I find it quite irritating to stand in line at a grocery store and hear babies cry for the candy, which is eye level to them at the check out counter. Mom thumbs through a magazine that she has no plans on buying while baby screams. So many times, I've wanted to gently tap Mom on the shoulder to let her know that her shopping buddy is bothered about something, and wants her attention. To date, I haven't done it, but I so desire to do it. I may get slapped or sued, so I'd better not.

It is my prayer that as I raise (rear, for those who don't like that word. But that's what we do in Athens, we raise children. Get over it!) my daughters, I hope that I can be all that my mama was and still is to me. I think I'm on the right track. My oldest daughter, Jordan, who is twelve, wrote a note to me that, among other things, said she loves me because I am strict but fair, and because I trust them. She doesn't realize that those words meant more to me than any Christmas gift, Mother's Day gift or anything else she could ever give. It reminded me of the respect and love that I have for my mother. We have a great relationship, and even though I tried a couple of silly tricks in my life, she never lost her trust in me. Unlike parents of today, my mother didn't go to any great lengths to be my friend. It was okay with her if I didn't like her. My birth certificate did not ask for a friend's name; it asked for my Mother's name.

Because Mama didn't "hang out" with too many people, she was a very private person, and those who don't know her can easily mistake her for being standoffish. I now wish I would have picked up on this valuable trait of hers, earlier in my life. She minds her own business, and doesn't give much value to what others deem important. Her priorities have always been her family and her job. That's why, when she bought me a Ford Mustang when I was only fifteen, she didn't care what others thought. After all, she was paying the bills, and in her words, "They don't run my house!" That's still how she views life. She does what she chooses to do for her children. While others may choose to call us spoiled, she says we are blessed. She believes that if she has something, and if her children are in need and she didn't help them, that is the sin of selfishness. Don't be deceived; she doesn't just go around doling out money and gifts for foolishness. Her rules were simple:

1. Go to jail, don't call me.

2. Come up pregnant, find somewhere else to live.

3. Act like you've got some sense, and I'll support you, all the way.

Because of that way of thinking, and her never negotiating on those three principles, we fully understood the rules of the house, and exactly what was expected from us at all times. (For the record, we never went to jail or became pregnant while living in her house.) Although I'm pretty sure that she would have still loved us if we broke one of the top three, I never felt stupid enough to test her to see if she was serious.

Over and over, she proved to my dad and the rest of the world that she shouldn't be taken lightly. The battery in her car lost its charge, and rather than getting a new battery, my daddy bought her a brand new car — one that she neither asked for, nor liked. She was livid! She did not accept his gesture of kindness. She refused to drive it, and walked to work every day for three weeks. He finally gave in, and returned to the car dealership, this time, with his wife. He asked that she select the car she preferred. Even though they left with another new car, she took every liberty to remind him, "The car I had only needed a battery. This is *your* car, I want mine back." The car never came back and Daddy never tried to surprise her like that again. She still speaks up for what she wants and what she believes. She's my hero. Daddy always called her his "whippersnapper," the name that still fits her best. My mother is quite a woman, much like the virtuous woman in Proverbs 31. Her children rise and call her blessed, at least I do.

My daddy died when I was eleven. Even though he left me before I was ready, before I could ask him all the things daughters need to know, I learned a lot from this one-of-a-kind man. I learned how to love, try new things, and accept that everybody was not the same. He also showed me what a best friend will and will not do.

Daddy was a handsome fair-skinned brother with wavy *good* hair. I can imagine how when my mom took one look at him, she had to have fallen in love at first sight. He was just that handsome! The stature and look of Harry Belafonte, but all the charisma of Billy Dee Williams, fused with the tailored couture style of Steve Harvey. Yep, that's close to my daddy. He often told a story (unconfirmed, but very possible) of him marrying three women in one day. Of course, I hope it's not true, but if anyone could have pulled it off, it would have been him. Let's just put it like this, in his wilder and days prior to being tamed by my mother "The Fine Brown Frame," his Los Angeles nickname was Cadillac Red because he kept a new Caddy, and he was a pretty red man. Enough said? Can we move on now?

Daddy was a mathematical genius, a clever conversationalist, an avid outdoorsman, a hospitable entertainer, but would not go to church for love nor money. His mother passed away when he was only seven, and her father, Papa Newton Ewell, a Holy Ghost preacher from east Texas, assumed the responsibility of caring for my dad and his younger sister, Sook, (her nickname). So, as a child, Daddy went to church every day, everywhere, and could quote the scriptures better than any ordained minister today will ever be able to. But he still refused to go to church as an adult. He once told me, "I am a man of my word, and if I tell you I'm going to do it, I'm going to do it, but if I say I'm not doing it, you better believe it," he said. "I promised the Lord, if he ever got me out of Cuney, Texas, and more specifically, out of Papa's church, I'd never go back."

He meant it because as long as we lived, and as much as he loved me, his only baby girl, he never went to church with me. He made certain that I went each Sunday, but he wouldn't go. The only time he'd even think about going into a church was for a *family* funeral. He had already told his closest friends, "I'm telling you now, so your folks won't be upset, I'm not coming to your funeral when you die." And he didn't. But they came out by the hundreds for his home-going celebration.

Daddy had a mouth like a sailor; however, he never served in any branch of the armed services. He didn't care much for white people, either. He certainly had no problem telling them exactly what they could do for him. I don't know if he qualified as a racist, he just couldn't stand most white people. There were a few to make his A-list, but not many. I can remember him telling me, with a few colorful terms, "Patrice, when it comes to white folk, *use* them before they *use* you." (I'll let your imagination take you to the many not-so-nice words he could have said.) I can also remember Mama yelling from the kitchen, "Cliff, don't talk to her like that. Don't you ever use *that* word around her again." He thought it was the funniest thing he had ever said because he laughed all the way to the bedroom. But that's okay, I remembered what he said, and with distinct clarity. Now, at the age of thirty-six, I chuckle thinking about his warning to me, and wondering how my life would have differed, if I had taken his advice on Dealing with White Folk 101.

As I mentioned, he was quite the entertainer, and often invited his white friends to our small 1,100 square foot home, "across the divide" for dinner. All would graciously accept his invitation. But he said he didn't trust some of them outside the walls of our home. Without fail, his friends would rave about Mama's great cooking. When they'd leave, he'd say something silly like, "Sorry S.O.B., probably gon' go home and beat his wife, because she can't cook." It gave him great joy to show off his wife and his baby girl. He did it all the time, every chance he got…even with total strangers.

One afternoon as he entered a service station to pay for gas in Tyler, he struck up a conversation with another store patron, who happened to be a pilot for one of the major airlines, who was on a layover for two days.

{Press PAUSE} You are safe to assume that based on his occupation, he was not of the Negroid species. {Press PLAY, please}.

Without knowing anything about the man, *Cadillac Red* invited him to stay at our house and forget about the hotel room that his company had already paid for.

"Man, my wife will cook up a good meal for you, and you can drive back tomorrow night, if you want to," Daddy encouraged.

So, the man took Daddy up on his offer, and went home with him. Of course, my mother wanted to beat Daddy upside the head with the broom, as he walked in with the uniformed stranger following close behind him.

Instead, she welcomed the man into our small home, and prepared a bed for him. The dinner she made that night was outstanding, and I know this based on the way he seemed to crouch over his plate, so as not to miss a drop of gravy from the smothered steak. He enjoyed the dinner he ate with us that night. He stayed a day, and flew out two days later, as planned. I don't know if Daddy ever heard from him again, but I'm sure, wherever he is, he never forgot his encounter with that tall slender fellow from Athens, who didn't care for people not like him, but loved inviting them into his home...just to see how the "other side of the tracks" really lived.

Even though we loved television's Evans family, not every black family lived in a tenement, like Jay-Jay, Thelma & Michael from Good Times. Nor did all black men reside in a junk yard, as our favorite grouch, Fred Sanford did.

"When water was free, ghetto was where people lived; not how they acted."

My daddy was more of the George Jefferson type, outspoken, could not be outdone, and out to be heard. We never "moved on up to our deeeeluxe apartment in the sky," but Daddy made everyone feel like we had nothing but the best.

There was nothing more fun than eating tacos with him. He didn't quite pronounce it like everyone else. He called them, "tockas." And we had some of my best memories eating "tockas" at the Dairy Queen in Athens, after he'd pick me up from school.

Lake Athens was my private playground. While other children were remanded to their homes after school to spend the afternoon watching "I Love Lucy" and "Brady Bunch" re-runs, Daddy and I would spend the evening in our boat, the Miss Kiss which was named for me. He would pick me up from school, towing the boat, and I knew we would spend the day on the calm waters of the lake. At the marina, we'd buy two dozen minnows; one dozen for him, another dozen for me to "lose" while I perfected my skills as a junior angler. He'd order us a hamburger, a good greasy hamburger, potato chips and two orange sodas, for our evening snack.

My job was guiding the boat off the trailer, as Daddy backed the truck down the ramp. After parking the truck, he'd return to the ramp to crank Miss Kiss up, and we'd start our adventure. Once out of the view of the marina (and the game warden), I'd take the wheel, and engage the throttle full speed ahead. Daddy let me do whatever I wanted. My two ponytails flapped in the wind, as I bounced the boat across the waves. Daddy would occasionally nod his head in agreement that I was doing a good job as the captain.

He would point out a particular cove on the lake, and there, we would lower the anchor (a recycled gallon milk jug filled with cement) until the fish stopped biting. If I had homework, we did it together while Daddy fished, and I polished off the hamburger. He could keep a minimum of four fishing rods baited and in the water at a time. Not me. I liked casting – according to him, "wasting good bait." I mastered the art of crappie fishing and could snag one in the roof of its mouth as well as any of Daddy's other buddies could. He always reminded me, "Patrice, there are two things white folk will never be able to do like black folk....catch crappie and cook barbecue. It just won't happen."

Other than the occasional buzz of a mosquito, the lake was always quiet, and a good place to relax from the stresses of elementary school. It was on one of our Lake Athens outings that Daddy asked me about my career goals.

"Patrice, what do you want to be, when you grow up?"

"I 'on't know, Daddy."

"You ever thought about being a nurse, like your mama?" I knew the answer to that was no. I had practically grown up in a nursing home because sometimes I'd go to work with Mama. As a result, at the age of nine, some of my best friends were in their nineties. Not cute.

"No, sir, I don't want to be a nurse," I answered.

"You know what I think you'd be really good at?" He urged.

"No. What? A secretary?"

"No, baby, not a secretary. You'll be the first black woman as President of these United States."

"For real, Daddy? Me?" I shrieked.

When water was free, it was a compliment to be considered intelligent enough to become President of the United States.

"Yeah, girl. You can do it. First thang you've gotta do is go to law school."

"I gotta be a lawyer, first?"

"Not really, but it'll be a good start for you. As long as there are crooks like Richard Nixon around, you'll never be out of work."

I probably should have followed my daddy's suggestion because I've got so much of him in me that I can put up a pretty good argument with the best of them. I would have been a pretty decent attorney. Instead, nine years after his death, and completely bored with junior college, Ms. Pac Man and playing pool, I moved to Dallas/Ft. Worth. I entered the once-upon-a-time glamorous travel industry. For the record, I am still arguing with people for a living. This time, I argue trying to convince others that I do not have the inside track; nor do I have the "hook up" to get discounted or free tickets; and the low fare requires twenty one days advance purchase and a Saturday night stay. I should have listened to my daddy.

I knew I would have to stop telling people about my line of work, when I was at church and another congregant did an approximate 180 degree turn to ask "Do you know how much it would cost to go to Los Angeles?" {Please press Pause} I was in church; no computer access, no dates of travel, no clue as to anything, just my sermon notes. {Press Play} I wanted to say, "Turn around and look at the monitors. You're on the big screen asking me for a ticket and everybody sees you." But, I kindly smiled and sent her my business card, and asked that she call me the next day. I never heard from her again.

That incident made me wonder, do other people get accosted the same way in their relative fields? I don't think so. I don't see people walking up to a dentist, who they just meet, and slinging their heads back with open mouths to show their new acquaintance that tooth way back there in the back that has been bothering them. Or do total strangers walk up to insurance salespeople to inquire, "What's the bad weather gon' do to premiums next year? I have yet to see people going up to policemen to ask, "Do you know how much time I can get if I rob somebody?" Have you? So, why, why, why have people singled me out? Why? Huh? Why?

The world was mine, for the asking. All I had to do was ask my daddy. On a trip to the bank with him, and while I sat there waiting for him, I watched as the bank teller typed. I had seen typewriters at school, but never really watched anyone type. The fact that the lady could type so quickly without ever looking at the keys amazed me. I had to have a typewriter, just like hers. I casually mentioned it to Daddy as we drove away. That night, he came home with a Smith Corona electric typewriter, just like the one at the bank. I was seven years old. Spoiled, you say? No, I've said it before, I prefer blessed. That's what my mama taught me. I soon learned that typing wasn't as easy as it looked. But for the first couple...okay, okay, maybe eight years...I just typed....and typed fast! No, you couldn't read anything that I typed, but I was doing just like the lady at the bank. I still have the typewriter, but it's mine and no one can have it because my superhero gave it to me. Funny, my children have no idea what it is or how to use it. Yet, they type around thirty words per minute at ten and twelve years old.

When water was free, our heroes were superheroes — men who by day, sported a suit to work, and when trouble arose, they quickly transformed into super human strength donning tights and a cape to save humanity from evil, but returned to work.

Did you catch that? Superheroes had day jobs. Superman, Spiderman, Wonder Woman and the Incredible Hulk all had W-2s on file with the IRS, as employees. Half the reason Superman was faster than a speeding bullet, was his work ethic. He didn't want to be late for work. Today's heroes aren't super anymore, as most don't have a day job. They are multi-millionaire athletes and entertainers, and that's their only gig.

Don't get me wrong, there are still a few superheroes around. Men and women who have more than one job and are willing to put in a little extra time. Please consider that we no longer call him, Magic Johnson, NBA Superstar; he's now Mr. Earvin Johnson, CEO, Philanthropist and Entrepreneur. At one time in his life, he was only known for his mesmerizing abilities on the hardwoods. Now, he's seated at the head of the table in corporate boardrooms. Yes, that's a superhero. At a gala held recently in Dallas honoring Mr. Johnson, he commented, "I'm not doing anything special; I'm doing what I am supposed to do." [Giving back to the communities who made him the icon he was.] Mr. Johnson, keep up the great work, and please encourage our other brothers and sisters to do so.

I must now clarify my earlier statement. "The world was mine for the asking," except for a calculator. As I mentioned earlier, Daddy was a brilliant mathematician. I made the mistake of asking for a calculator once. It was the only time I asked for one. Here's why. I quickly realized that I probably would have done better by asking him to go to church with me. He went off, and ranted and raved for seemingly no less than thirty minutes about how those silly little machines would make people lazy.

"You won't think. You won't need to because you'll have a machine doing it for you! You won't challenge your mind; you'll just accept what it says and go on with your life. You'll be like everybody else. You'll be just another *that'll do Negro*. If you settle for a calculator, you'll settle for anything." He continued his speech. "You've gotta be twice as sharp as white people to beat them at their game, and if you've got a calculator working for you, you won't think for yourself. People will be able to tell you anything and you'll believe it. You won't think for yourself. You'll get lazy, just like everybody else. Nobody likes lukewarm coffee, Patrice."

"To hell with that, Patrice. You've got a brain, I expect you to use it."

This went on for about two minutes, but it seemed like days. Coming from a man who could take a four-digit number and multiply it by another four-digit number, in his head…no pencil or paper required, I learned my lesson. His loving tirade ended when he told me "As long as I'm alive, don't you ever ask me for one of those d*** things again. Now come and give me some sugar!"

I said, "Okay" and as I hopped into his lap, and thought to myself, *I bet I won't ever do that again.*

But, boy, almost twenty-five years later, I must admit he was so right. Sure enough, after he died, I never applied myself in mathematics, anymore. I didn't have to. He wasn't around anymore to make sure that I was *thinking*. My report cards proved that I had no desire to associate in any way with numbers, in theory or in practice. This fear is still evident today, as I am terrified of math. Who knows? Probably beneath this dreadful terror, there probably is a junior mathematics expert, just like my daddy. Nevertheless, I never asked for another calculator....until after March 2, 1980, the day he died.

Despite what the world says about weapons of mass destruction, or handgun laws, or homeland security, there was never a safer place on earth than in my daddy's lap. There was nobody big and bad enough to mess with me, as long as my daddy was around. I will love him forever and no one else compares to that gentle giant. Labron Walker comes in as a close second. (He's my father-in-law and I love him dearly.)

***

Of the seven children born to Ruben and Ruth Jordan, all were "fruitful and multiplied." Our family now proudly boasts more than 140 brothers, sisters, nieces, nephews, uncles, aunts and cousins. There are so many cousins we can't count them all. Let's just say we, The Tribe of Jordan, will have our own section in heaven reserved for the cousins. There are so many of us, there are some who we only know by nickname. There's Nay-Nay, Jay-Jay, Nat, Popeye, Pre Sweet, Nikki, Mother (not my mama, this is a cousin, younger than me) Billy and Billy, Mimi (but that's her real name), Goo-Goo, D. J., Pooh, Sissy, Andy, and Teedy. That's me. And as far as the pronunciation of my nickname, it's TEE DEE, nothing else. (There are two Billy's, six Ruben's, four Ruth's, four Marie's, two Bernard's and two Jordan's in our family, and when you call one of them, any combination of them may answer.) Of course, everyone has given names, but the majority of "the tribe" doesn't know them. We pointed this out at our most recent family reunion, when we played our family version of Who Wants to be a Millionaire, "What's That Child's Real Name?"

And then there are the family friends, those who have been around so long, they are now "play cousins": Nene, Tanya, Venita, Lillie Bell, Brother, (not my brother, Venita and Lillie Bell's brother), Twanna, Squeaky, Ivie, Carla and Pam and anybody else who has been around us for years. If they aren't at the family gatherings, they are missed.

When water was free, everybody was family, and you didn't need an invitation to a family reunion. You didn't even need to be family; you just needed to show up.

Sunday was always a family day. No need to rush and do anything, but go to church. Church was church. It was the family experience. Even those who had no biological family could always depend on the church family. Your social position did not matter; instead, the concern was for your heart condition. Church was the one opportunity to relax from the week's worries, and concentrate on the Lord's heavenly promises.

When water was free, you didn't have to audition for the church choir. It was simple, if you could sing, the choir needed you. If you couldn't sing, then you needed the choir.

My grandmother was the pianist for our children's choir, so, at minimum, the choir stand was full of her grandchildren.

When water was free, we did not have a pianist and a choir director.

The pianist was the director. She simply threw her hand up to have us stand, and nodded her head at the person when it was time to sing. When the song was over, she used that same hand or a nod of her head to tell us to be seated. It worked well, and didn't cost the church any extra tithes or offering.

It has been said that back in the day, in the early days of our church, if something had gone awry at the church business meeting on Monday evening, that on the following Sunday, Granny would take her pocketknife out of her purse and use it as a prop for her hymnal. She left it out as she played the piano, just to keep everybody in check. I guess she was simply obeying God's word, and working toward her heavenly blessing. His word says, "Blessed are the peacemakers..."

Going to church every Sunday was not an option for me. Mama's rule was quite simple: If you woke up on Sunday morning, you were going to church — to your church, not your friend's church, but your own. However, if you died during the night, you'd be getting prepared for your funeral service later in the week. Simply stated, one way or the other, you were going to church that week...alive or dead. Even as I reached the age of being able to go out on Saturday night, Em's rule did not change. "You can party all night, if you want to, but at 9:45 in tha morning, you better be at the secretary's table in Sunday school, fulfilling your duties...sleep or awake. You better be there! Like clockwork, I was there. Many times I was half asleep, but I was there to count the money and record the minutes.

The old deacons would sing "Guide Me O, Thou Great Jehovah" to begin the Sunday services. Everybody knew, when the song began, it was time to get situated and quiet. During that time we'd finish filling out the tithing envelopes, get our change out for *penny offering* and conclude last minute conversations. It was your last chance to spit out the grape Bubble Yum in your mouth. Ms. Lena, the head usher, didn't care that you just bought it. "Spit it out, rat here in this envelope...rat now," she would say. There was no place for it in church, and it wasn't in the Bible, so you'd better spit it out on your own, or expect her finger in your mouth to fish it out! (I always opted for the voluntary removal.)

I can remember how the deacons — much older than deacons today — would pray with one knee on the floor, and their elbow propping their bowed head, as they knelt on a chair for support. The more they prayed, the more the "amen corner" hummed and moaned.

"Hebmly fotha, it's once mo' anduh gin jussa few o yo humba suhrvants stopped by yo house to seh thank ya fo' anutha week's jurnie. Lawt...you been mighty, mighty good. Right now, we jess wonna seh thank ya for anutha chaince to come out an wisship you in spirt an in trufe. Right now, most

Holy, we want askyo blessin upon dis house. My lawd go to the harspittle and to the nussing home, cool scorchin' feevas, ease rackin pains. Watch over the widdas and the orffens. Fuhgive us lawd frum ouva evil sins. Clean us out lawd, till you clean ussup, lawd. Hebmly fotha, Mary's little baybeh. Oh my fotha! Hep us lawd, to do dose thangs pleasing in yo sight. Keep us mindful of yo bidness, my lawd. And masta, when we come to the enda this jurnie, and evva thang we can do on this side is done been done, give us a happy ouva in death, so we can praise yo name fuh ever, and ever, Aaymen."

That's how church started.

While we are on the subject, where has the amen corner gone? The mothers of the church, who coined the term, "*mission Sunday.*" On the first Sunday they provided the bread and juice for communion, and we loved it because the bread was homemade. The goofy kids that we were, our feelings were often hurt when we weren't given the leftovers. (We didn't have a clue that it was sacred, and not for our greed and hunger.)

When water was free, you could easily find the mothers of the church dressed in their white suits and hats, and NOBODY had on spandex.

I'm sorry. Spandex just ain't a sacred fabric. Leave it at home, please.

I didn't know it then, but I was saved because I had confessed Jesus as my savior. I believed He was the son of God and that God raised him from the dead. But if you had asked me if I was saved, I would have emphatically (and ignorantly) told you "no."

Those saved people, the Holiness people, you know, the Church of God in Christ folks, were not like me. They went to those little churches with the drums and tambourines, and shouted and spoke in tongues. Their girls couldn't wear pants or shorts, and never wore makeup. They couldn't go to school dances. So no, I was not saved. Twenty something years later, I know I'm saved, but am more aware of the measure of my salvation, and no devil in hell can tell me any different.

Family reunions were, and still are, enough fun to last us for a year. It almost takes a year for us to work off the extra calories. Saturdays are full of fun, as the family drives in from all around Texas to chat, play dominoes, take a chance at the piñata, and eat.

When water was free, French wine was called, Andre Cold Duck. Birthday celebrations and outdoor family gatherings called for domestic wines, straight from Boone's Farms.

I'll stop here to let the Super Saints catch their breaths. Yes, at least three times a year, there was some call for celebration. That's when Mama and Daddy would break out the "good stuff" to commemorate the occasion. Buying a case of the good stuff never set you back for more than twenty bucks. To toast a spectacular event, we were not worried about uncorking the finest bottle, but rather untwisting the tallest, greenest bottle sticking out of the paper bag. If there were a family gathering, there would always be a cooler of Cragmont sodas from Safeway for the kids, a cooler of beer for the adults and two or three bottles of Boone's Farm's finest. I couldn't wait until the day when I'd be able to taste it, for myself, or better yet, buy my own bottle. (Country Kwencher, Tickle Pink and Strawberry Hill were the preferred flavors.)

You couldn't have a gathering without the music, courtesy of Daddy's 8-track tapes. I can still hear Marvin Gaye singing "Keep on dancin'...got to give it up!" "My pride and joy....you pick me up when I'm down" and "How sweet it is to be loved by you...."

Anyone within a block could smell the smoke from Mama's three barbeque pits, and the pungent mystery of the secret cooking sauce she made.

Inside, the house was a buzz of excitement of kids running in and out for yet, one more slice of the African plum: watermelon. The recoiling "SCHLAPPPP" of the screen door was commonplace as kids ran in and out of the house. Those who weren't eating watermelon were sneaking into Mama's potato salad. We would lift the foil to stick our fingers into the salad, much like children who eat leftover cake batter. Mama's potato salad was best when you got a finger full of it, while nobody was looking. By the time she was ready to serve it, half the bowl was gone.

When water was free, dominoes was a bone-slapping, smack-talking game my daddy and uncles used to play. Today, it's who's cooking dinner.

Family, food, music and dancing... it all just went together, as long as nobody got drunk. If someone "took it to the limit," they had to leave, with explicit instruction from my daddy. (Remember his mouth?)

Now, it's the twenty-first century and we have stepped up and learned that a good wine needs good legs. (That's funny to me; I never knew smashed grapes had body parts.) We know that a good Pinot Noir is bold with flavor, and that a Chardonnay is great with white meat. According to my family, so was Boone's Farms. Now, you don't blink an eye as you authorize your platinum Visa card for a $200 bottle of Dom Perignon.

Some of you don't. I do. If I want something bubbly, Sprite with a twist of lemon does the trick for me, without the headache that follows a flute of champagne.

Exactly when did fried chicken wings become the finger food of choice? Nobody knows. Now, don't get me wrong, I love hot wings. But in a recent conversation with a few of my closest friends, I asked the question. My peers and I came up blank, as we sought to provide the correct answer. When and how did they become so popular?

When water was free, fried chicken wings were a staple for blacks, colored, or whatever we were then. Anyway, they were the main course for Sunday dinner, especially if we had a three o'clock evening service that day.

You could expect to have fried chicken wings, mashed potatoes and pork and beans, for two reasons: They were cheap and quick to prepare. Now, you can't go anywhere without "wingz" as the number one appetizer offered. The y2k4 wings are dressed differently, however. They now come in teriyaki, honey mustard, Cajun, hot, hot-hot, and Satan's spit hot. There are as many sauces available for dipping, as there are varieties of flavors. Ranch dressing, barbecue sauce, gravy, honey mustard, and so on.

When water was free, the only dipping sauce with fried chicken wings was KETCHUP. So, what's up with ranch dressing? When did it make its debut? When water was free, we grew up on Kraft Catalina dressing, and I ate my share as a child so that my kids won't have to. They're "ranch" girls.

How silly are we to pay $6 for ten chicken wings? Do we really think about what we are spending our money on? The boniest, cheapest part of the boniest, cheapest meat available? While you are answering that one, can you please let me know what a "drummette" is? Does it come from a "chickenette"? Whatever the case, like many of you, I will stand in line to get an order of wings with ranch dressing. My daddy must be turning over in his grave.

I have always felt God made bananas for his precious little monkeys, and He made pork and beans for black folk. We love 'em. My mother ate them right out of the can when she was pregnant with me. This probably helps you to understand why I like them, too. I have yet to meet someone who doesn't like them. And if you don't like pork and beans, chances are we probably won't get off to a great start. I've even seen people mix pork and beans with their whole kernel corn. Shamed to say it, but I tried it and it was good. Ugly, but good. First, they are versatile and go with everything. I've mentioned fried chicken. Now, when we would have a cookout, Mama would add barbecue sauce, chopped onions and peppers, brown sugar, a smidgen of mustard and put them into a 350 degree oven. They then became *baked* beans. When payday was still two days away, we cut up a weenie or two, put them in with the beans, and had *beanie weenies*. You can't go wrong with pork and beans, the most versatile bean around.

Secondly, you know they are for us because of that one little piece of pork that's in them. We all know that everything is better with a little piece of fat in it – turnip greens, cabbage, black-eyed peas and pork and beans.

{Please press PAUSE.} For all of the health enthusiasts, my hats go off to you. I applaud your commitment to "keeping the temple, holy and acceptable." But again, this ain't Healthy Cooking 101. This, in case you have forgotten, is a look back at when water was free. We *all* grew up on pork and beans. And back then, the more fat meat, the better. {Press PLAY}

Finally, pork and beans were an acceptable excuse for bad manners for children like me who loved them so much. I could always say, "Ma, it was all those beans I ate!" Go ahead and laugh; it's okay. If you've eaten as many pork and beans as I have, you know what I'm talking about. If you haven't, then you have missed out on a great gastronomic life experience.

Once I went out for dinner with a smooth Kappa Alpha Psi brother, and he was not just another pretty one. Brother man had it going on! Of course, he was pretty. Not handsome;

he was pretty! (It seems like most of them have to be, in order to become a brother of the diamond, but not always.)

He was well spoken and very well dressed. He was a debonair, southwestern version of Will Smith. He reminded me very much of my daddy's size and demeanor, with the same broad, strong shoulders as my daddy, and "slack in the back" just like him, too. But he didn't talk like Daddy, thank God. This man was smoove (yes with the "v"). As expected, he opened the car door for me, pulled my chair out as we were seated for dinner, and that was the start of a night that will always be remembered. He presented me with flowers, as he commented on how this night was the start of a great beginning for us. I was absolutely blinded by the twinkle in his eye, as he looked my way. After taking my order, the waiter listened as he ordered his entrée. The waiter asked, "What side items would you prefer?" He asked, "What do you offer?" The waiter replied with a list of five or six options, and what my pretty K A Psi man said, I'll never forget.

"I'll take the beans."

"Which beans?" the waiter inquired.

He looked up at the waiter and with that Kappa razzle-dazzle still in his eye, he answered, "Porkin."

After I excused myself to the ladies room, I couldn't contain my laughter, as hard as I tried. I knew this had to be special because he, too, knew the goodness of my favorite bean.

Now, in 2004, in the aftermath of the worse terrorism to ever touch U.S. soil, our nation reeled as the economy was capsized by the attacks on September 11, 2001. As people lost jobs and struggled to make ends meet, I was pleasantly amazed to see a Caucasian woman doing her best to get to the pork and bean aisle at my neighborhood Albertson's grocery store. The advertisement had them listed at ten cans for one dollar. I couldn't even get to the beans for the white people. What was the world coming to? Could it be that they now knew our secret? Was she the one to grab the last package of neck bones before I could get to them?

Now, here's the irony about my love for pork and beans. Just to the right of my favorite brand of pork and beans, there was a new name in town. BUSH's beans! Is this George W and family? Do they now want a piece of the bean pie, too?

Sunday's dinner on the grounds meant that everybody brought a covered dish, and ate together. None of this one can of corn business that we call fellowship, today. No, when the kitchen committee decided it was time to stir up some excitement, you could expect to eat until you could eat no more. You could bring your own foil because there was always enough to take extras home.

If you have seen the movie "Soul Food," you know where I'm going with this. For those who haven't seen it, come with me to fellowship hall of Mt. Providence Baptist for a glimpse at dinner after church. Just imagine if a church fellowship hall had a kitchen table. (The kitchen table, because the dining room table is reserved for desserts.) On the table, you'd find every possible way you can cook a chicken... smothered, stewed, baked, barbecued, fried, and the list goes on. In the oven, there's a turkey and a pot roast cooking side by side. Who would have ever thought a cow and a bird, could co-exist in the same environment?

On the "eyes" of the stove (burners, for those of you who aren't from east Texas), there are cream peas, black-eyed peas, purple-hulled peas, collard, turnip, and mustard greens, with a signature ham hock simmering on top. On the kitchen counter is a squash casserole, homemade macaroni and cheese, candied yams, fried corn, fresh green beans, cabbage, cornbread, a hen and dressing, ham (that's glazed with orange soda), and potato salad. The beverage of choice was tea, sweet tea or tropical punch Kool-Aid. My granny called it "poly pop." By now, you see that this kind of food nourishes and fills the body and the soul. Life was easy then.

When water was free, people didn't have a stroke about their high cholesterol or high blood pressure from high intake of pork.

That's how it was, and that's how we ate. Everybody from east Texas knows that when your *pressure* went up, a good tablespoon of vinegar would do the trick.

Now, let's go on to the dessert table. A three-layer German chocolate cake, tall butter pound cake, strawberry cake with strawberry Kool-Aid icing, 7up cake, coconut cake, pineapple upside-down cake and Italian crème cake are all lined up. Mena always talked about how tall the cakes were then, suggesting that you'd need a step ladder to step up just to cut one of them. Banana pudding, buttermilk pie, lemon cheese pie, pecan pie also have great representation on the temptation table.

For anyone who wants it, there's a metal water cooler, with the sweetest, purest water God ever made — Athens water. But then again, just about everything from Athens was sweet and pure, the food, the folks and the love.

After church, all of the kids would head for Pete's candy store, and then to North Park, for a day of music and baseball.

When water was free, every adult had a title before his or her name — Mr., Miss, Auntie, Uncle or Cousin — except Pete.

Pete was the candy man in Athens, and old enough to be everybody's granddaddy. Kids from all over town walked to his one-room candy store, where a dollar could buy you enough junk to last a week. Every chocolate candy bar imaginable was stocked behind his Plexiglas candy case. Pixy sticks, chic-o-sticks, grasshopper candies, Jolly Ranchers, cinnamon rolls, powdered donuts; you name it, Pete had it. Apple Now and Laters, a pickle with a peppermint stick, moon cookies, and a Nehi grape soda were a few of my favorites. It was pretty cool to call him by his name, and even cooler that he didn't mind.

While walking, one group would meet up with another group, and by the time you made it to the park, you were one of about twenty groups of people walking down Red Hill toward North Park. This was the one place where everyone could get together, listen to music, watch a softball game and just hang out. No fights, no drama, and no police, until they got bored. But even when they'd get bored, they would drive through the park and not bother us. After all, we were not drinking, smoking or being unruly. That's when having fun was simple.

Chapter

3 "I Won't Complain"

Around our way holidays and funerals are always a time of rejoicing. Many don't understand how we can laugh through our grieving, but that's just as much a part of who we are, as the not so healthy, but oh so satisfying feasts we devour at those times. Trust me; something is bound to happen during a funeral. No matter how serious or how reverent we are, something happens. We all laugh about it, usually after the crowds are gone. Please do not misunderstand me. The death of a loved one is never a laughing matter. And for some, bearing a smile is the most difficult thing to do because of the unrelenting pain associated with a broken heart. Your heart is broken. Your emotions are overcharged, and your future has changed forever.

It is not my suggestion that you laugh at death. After it's all over, the funeral, the food and all the people are gone, instead of focusing on the deafening silence booming around us, and rather than tuning in to the void that now occupies our hearts, we remember the best times, the funniest times. If necessary, we recall the silliest thing our loved one ever did. When you grieve, I encourage you to do the same, and smile until you chuckle to yourself. Replace tears of grief with those of joy. These tears feel better on your face and they aren't nearly as salty. Go ahead, taste one...just like you did when you were a kid. Nobody's looking...go on.

At my granny's funeral in 1988, as we lined up for the processional, her younger sister, Aunt Thelma, who was the first diva in the family, suffered from Alzheimer's disease (Or as people in east Texas say, "Old Timer's" disease). While approaching the steps of the church, we whispered to her that it was time to go in, but she was not ready. So, we waited another few minutes for her and still she wasn't ready. By that time our other surviving great aunt, Chunky, grew tired of waiting. So she pinched Aunt Thelma to gently persuade her to step it up. Louder than the minister who read Psalms 23, and still louder than the small choir who sang the words, "Be not dismayed, whate'er be tide, God will take care of you," Aunt Thelma screamed, "Ouch, Chunky, you're hurting me!"

And that started it. We laughed all the way up the steps and into the church until the ushers had seated us. For the first ten minutes of the service, we all took turns leaning down into the pew toward the floor to disguise the chuckles, which had consumed us. The ushers thought we all had been overcome with grief, and they ran to our sides, with tissues in hand to comfort us. Little did they know that the tears we were wiping were of laughter, and certainly not sorrow, yet. We made it through Granny's funeral fine, but Aunt Thelma helped make it easier for us.

I can recall attending a funeral with my youngest daughter, Jamie, who was three years old at the time, and quite observant. She decided during the time of the final viewing of the deceased that she did not want to go. Like an old lady whispering behind a fan, she said to me, "Mommy, I don't want to go look at that thing." (I assumed she was referring to the casket.)

I leaned over to her and whispered, "That's all right, you don't have to. I'll stay here with you."

She said, "Okay, good, because it must be something scary in that thang 'cause when everybody goes up there to look in, they start screaming!" And with that, she pulled her feet up into the pew, and managed to stand up to direct the people on the other side of us to cross over because we weren't moving. I knew then, she'd make somebody's church a great usher.

Let's talk about the people who take it upon themselves to give unsolicited remarks about the deceased and then clear their throat to announce, "I've got a song in my spirit, and y'all pray for me, while I try to sang it." They slide into their rendition of an unsolicited selection. Then, without warning, someone passes out. Kerrrplunk! They hit the floor — big ole hat, handkerchief, purse and all. They've been slain in the spirit!

That's a phenomenon I still don't understand, and in my Baptist innocence, it almost scared me to death, the first time I saw it happen. I forgot about what was going on, and worried that we'd have to make plans for another funeral. After taking Bible classes at my church, I still don't know exactly what's going on down there on the floor. I have not seen or read where Jesus ever slew anyone; instead, he raised people. When he laid his hands on people, they were renewed, not slewed. (That's not a word, but it rhymed. No, I'm not related to Jesse Jackson. And yes, this is still *my* book.) I even had the pleasure of working for a faith healing televangelist who admitted that he doesn't know why people fall; but that doesn't stop him from doing it. He keeps right on touching them, and they keep right on falling.

Someone laid hands on me, and when I didn't fall, they helped me by punching me right in the gut. You can bet I fell then. I didn't understand what was expected of me because I had not been exposed to it. It was almost like she was simulating WWF wrestling because she had me in a GI Joe Kung Fu grip about my head, and pushed me backwards toward the first row of chairs in the auditorium. When I didn't fall, well, you know the rest. I can honestly say that she never got that chance again, and I am more reluctant to let anyone lay hands on me. If I need hands, I've got two of my own, and I'll lay them on myself. If I'm ill, I'll call the elders of the church, (James 5:14) and if they can't pray for me, and my pastor can't get a prayer through, my deductible on my health insurance is only $250.00. But I'll be more prepared, and forever cautious, if I ever have anyone else do that to me again.

But then again, I'm just giving my conservative Southern Baptist born and bred perspective. In a world where everybody is something, but sometimes ashamed to be Baptist, I proudly tell the world I am a Baptist – a proud, platinum level water Christian. There are some who will be offended by that statement, but I'm sorry, love me anyhow, and pray for me (the weak) and remember…it's my book.

Once again from the mouth of my youngest daughter, Jamie, I learned that perhaps in my Baptist pride, I had forgotten to share with her, the basis of our beliefs. Rushing into the house after a December day in kindergarten, she asked me, "Mommy, where's our menorah?"

"Our what?" (I had no clue about what she was saying.)

"Our menorah and the driedel, you know mommy, for Hanukkah."

Talk about feeling silly. My baby thought we were Jewish. Here I was, "the church lady incarnate," and I had not shared with my children who we are in the family of God. I spent a few minutes talking to her about it, and everything was fine.

Now, back to the person on the floor. Not to worry because as soon as the person hits the floor, the ushers swarm into action, like a professional S.W.A.T. team. It's like the head usher gives an audible command. "You two, take sector one on the floor, and you two, to the front row, with one of you on either end so the family doesn't see what's going on. The rest of you grab some fans and execute plan "Fan Resuscitation." With meticulous and almost choreographed precision, they take control of the funeral. The sector one ushers hover, with their fans working. Sector two ushers take their position, protecting and serving, and within minutes, the person is revived. In all my years of churching, I haven't figured out exactly what is in those fans that can revive people, but whatever it is, it works. When the ushers have hoisted the person up from the floor, they check themselves to ensure that their suits are back in place, their badges straight, gloves are back on, and short of slapping each other a high-five, they resume their posts on the floor. I can give this narrative with authority because I am an usher at my church. (www.mesquitefriendship.com/ministries/usher).

If you've never seen what I've just described, it's worth going to a couple of "our folks" funerals, and you'll find out just what I'm talking about. If you've seen it, then you know I'm right.

So, here's something to write down and remember when my home-going service rolls around, and someone gets up to sing, without being asked to do so. You have my permission to do the right thing, on my behalf. Politely stand up, with your index finger raised toward heaven in reverence to Baptists everywhere, and with your head respectfully bowed, (while trying to restrain your laughter) say these words as loudly as your little gut can bellow, "Patrice said, sit down!"

Remember Aunt Thelma, the first diva in our family? Her story is worth telling as well (because I'm starting to feel a little "Thelma-ish" now that I realize the invaluable importance of family). She had to be our family's ebony-inspired version of Audrey Hepburn. If there were ever a mocha supreme version of Jacqueline Kennedy Onassis, her name would be Thelma Bernice Criner, my granny's sister.

Aunt Thelma was the picture of status and comfortable living when living in the third ward of Houston, Texas on Blodgett Street was prestigious. "Ted," as her husband called her, was often found lounging in the finest pink silk pajamas, with the matching robe and house slippers. And these were no plain-Jane robes and slippers. No Sir. They were trimmed in marabou feathers that gracefully swayed as she pranced about her Prima Diva kind of way.

If the casual urge for nicotine came to her, the paper butt of a cigarette never tasted her caramel kissed lips. When she opted to smoke a cigarette, she did so with the use of a rhinestone-encrusted cigarette holder. Diamonds were her best friends, but she shared them. She was downright classy and graceful in everything she did. Love and diamonds were hers to give to anyone who came within a reasonable distance to her. (I am wearing an antique diamond ring, now over sixty years old, which she gave to my mother over forty years ago.)

Many evenings, after finishing a gourmet meal, she'd be in her living room, seated at her baby grand piano, playing along with whatever tunes that happened to be on the TV. (The big wood grain floor model television/stereo console. Remember that? It was as long as a sofa and you lifted the top to control the stereo?) From time to time, she'd give us an impromptu concert, and encourage her fans (us kids) to sing along with her. The last one I can recall was her playing and singing, "Feelings, nothing more than feelings." She also played classical music, and taught piano lessons to anybody's children who would sit there on the stool with her.

Whenever we decided to make the trip down south, not just one household went, but two, maybe three different households would go together. That's how she liked it. The more was definitely the merrier at the Criner house.

Aunt Thelma's house was really neat to all of us because she was the only one in the family who had a two-story home at that time. Not only was it two stories, but the mailbox was built right into the house. The postman only needed to raise the flap outside, and push the mail through the slot, into the living room. The mailbox was the only thing to cause problems among the kids. We would all fight over who would get to gather the mail and bring it to her. Of course, she had a solution, which made everybody happy. She would take us outside, and each person had to take turns being the mailman, while somebody else on the inside received the mail. So, we did, and it worked without fail...Go 'head, Ted. How could she know that much about parenting, having never had children of her own?

No, she never gave birth to children of her own, but my generation all agrees that she was, by far, the family favorite. It didn't matter what anybody's name was, because all of the girls were called, "Baby" and all the boys "Bratha." (That's brother with a short "a" like lather, but bratha.) There were no rules at Thelma's house, except hers. Mamas and Daddies didn't matter. "Ted" was in control. And we all loved it — the kids as well as the parents.

No matter what time we would drive up at her home, she was ready to entertain. She cooked and fed everybody, all night long. She sent the parents to bed for fear they would mess up her good time with her great nieces and nephews. If anyone wanted to dance, she would turn on the stereo, and start her own Soul Train line. I distinctly remember her telling us that she could do "The Bump" better than any of us, and she proved it many times. At the time I was only about seven or eight, one of the youngest of all the kids there. She was at least sixty-five, but she was always my dance partner. It didn't matter to her; she would dance with us as long as we wanted to.

Or, if we (the kids) wanted to sit in the middle of the floor to play cards, Old Maid or Crazy 8's, jacks or marbles, she sat there and played with us, all night long...often beating all of us. Is anyone still playing marbles and jacks with their kids, or have we all hired the electronic baby-sitters — video games?

One of her favorite whatnots (these may be called curios in your home, but we called them whatnots) was a bank that she called "the money grabber." When a coin was placed on the bank's sensor, an eerie hand, like that of a skeleton, would come up from the bottom, and rake the coin into the bank. After the initial shock of seeing the hand, all the kids loved it. She even financed the deal, so we could all take turns doing it. Everybody was given a dime, and like goofy kids, we all screamed every time it did it.

(There were always at least seven or eight kids, so seven or eight different screams.) Yeah, we were goofy.

And if we ever decided to go to sleep, she was the last one to go to bed. Or better stated, go to floor. She'd turn her living room in to a giant sleepover. Out of the linen closet, she brought out the blankets, pillows and quilts to make a room-sized pallet for all eight or nine of us to sleep on. When dancing and playing finally defeated us, she'd zonk out on the floor, right there with us.

Sunrise at the Criner house was as renewing as any revival service I can recall attending. She took the time to draw the curtains and open the blinds to let a little south Texas coastal sun shine through.

"Rise and shine. It's breakfast time," she'd announce, as she shuffled into the kitchen to start breakfast. Her breakfasts were not a ten-minute, bacon and egg and you're done. Although that may have been one of the many options available during breakfast, you could expect any of three varieties of meats, breads, cereal, and eggs, prepared Chéz Ted.

Some of you may not have the mental picture yet. Let's take a walk into Ted's 1970s-inspired kitchen. Here, you'd find a well-appointed workspace, with all the latest appliances. The refrigerator would be stocked with everything she'd need to feed her kids for the weekend. Her décor represented the style of the day — pristine turquoise-tiled countertops. The fresh scent of bleach in the air tickled the nose. Sheer drapery hung over the kitchen window, an AM/FM radio with a round dial selector was nearby, and a newly planted ivy in a plastic cup sat near the window sill. The black leather barstools were always neatly pulled up to the bar, before all the kids rearranged them while climbing up to watch her work her magic. We loved those bar stools because they had no back support on them, so we'd climb up and spin round and round until nauseated (or until somebody's mama heard us laughing and screaming as we took turns being the spinner).

Before they could stop us, Aunt Thelma would interject, "Let the kids play. They can't hurt anything. Let them alone, I said!" With a wink of her eye, she'd finish with, "Get outta my way, Baby. I wrote the book, and it didn't read like that!" That was her comical response to anything that she disagreed with. Then she would follow that up with, "Let's have some understanding," while shaking her size 2 hips and winking her eye again. As she laughed and continued cooking, we kept up our mischief.

In one pan, the ham slowly simmered. In another sausage and bacon cooked together. There was a pot of oatmeal, a steamer full of rice (which we ate for breakfast with butter and sugar) and in yet another pot, she would have grits for those who are repulsed by the thought of rice for breakfast. She would mix up homemade pancakes, make toast and biscuits, and eggs, any and every way you could possibly want them. Coffee, hot chocolate, orange, grape or grapefruit juice were our typical choices for beverages. She would even squeeze fresh orange juice for anyone who wanted it.

She didn't ask for anyone's approval or assistance because it was *Ted's* kitchen. Only after the kids' plates were fixed, she'd tell the adults, "Let's eat y'all." She would bless the food and pile the plates high with the morning's meal. She made certain everyone had enough to eat, and was not concerned with where we ate. In the kitchen, living room, bedrooms, she didn't mind. She never worried about us messing up her "good stuff". We were her family, and who was more deserving of her good stuff than us? No one, in her eyes.

After breakfast, she'd start a pot of gumbo for lunch. While the aroma was thick with the smell of onions, green peppers and garlic dancing in a hot skillet and oil, the kids looked on in amazement. Aunt Thelma would let us kids play with shrimp and crabs as she cleaned them in the sink. (Not me. I was scared of everything, and would usually end up getting chased around the house by an older cousin.) She made the best gumbo I can recall having ever eaten. It was also at her house that I first tasted stuffed crab. The only time I have ever eaten menudo was in her kitchen. She did her best at bringing some form of multicultural exposure to our family. Given the choice of a charbroiled breast of chicken with a summer medley of sautéed julienne vegetables at a fine eating establishment, my family would opt for Ted's smothered steak and a big ole bowl of red beans, cornbread and hot sauce. Or if a menu offered prime rib, *some of my folks* would ask "Which barbecue sauce comes with it?" I still don't know how successful she was. Lord knows she tried to introduce new things.

Her heavy, cherry wood dining table sat eight people, although there were only she and Uncle Toby. The finest silver and imported linens, always adorned the well-designed table. In the middle of the table sat a huge fruit bowl, stocked with the freshest fruits available. A kid needed only to ask her if they could have one. Whatever the kid ate, she'd eat one of the same variety. Nobody was ever alone, and there was always enough fruit for everybody.

It's such memories that made us all love her so much. Her home was the gathering place for everyone, even the little children. And as Alzheimer's invaded her body and robbed her of her memory, it didn't touch ours. We all remember her in her glory days. We remember the dance contests; the breakfasts, and the diva in the slippers. Nothing can ever take those memories away from us.

When water was free, she was a diva, before being a diva was cool.

{Press PAUSE, please} Can you do me a huge favor? When you get to heaven, if you see a demure little angel sporting a rhinestone-encrusted halo, whose long white robe is frocked with marabou feathers, and her golden slippers have a three-inch high heel on them, if she looks lost, would you direct her to our family's section of heaven? Although there's no more Alzheimer's in heaver, she may be lost and looking for her family. Chances are, she'll be with her two other sisters, one will be Chunky, the one who pinched her, and the other will be my granny, with her Baptist hymnal, and its famous placeholder, which may not make it through heaven's metal detector.{Press PLAY}

Chapter 4 "My Endless Love?"

"With this ring, I thee wed." The words a girl longs to hear. As a little girl I can remember fantasizing about the day I would come down the aisle in that beautiful white dress. Remember? By the time we were in high school, we had chosen our colors and our bridal party. When we got to college, we began the selection process. He had to look like....he had to drive a....he had to make...he had to understand. Wow! What pressure to put someone under who we are hoping will spend the rest of our days with us. I have since learned the heart warming feeling you get as a teenager,when "that special someone" calls your name, is usually gas, and will pass relatively quickly.

My situation was different when this man walked into my life. We met in 1983 when I was sixteen. He was seventeen, tall and skinny with a big Afro, and a smile that would melt the coldest heart. Our mutual cousin, Mena, introduced us. Let me explain. I'm related to her through her father; he was related to her through her mother. So, that's how it came to be. Mena had told me about him for years, "Girl, you've got to meet my cousin Martin. He is so cute!" Finally, I agreed to go with her to the family reunion to see what all the excitement was about. My first glance at him was met with his charming and innocent smile. Yep, he was just as cute as she said he was.

What a family they have — aunts, uncles, cousins and food, everywhere. There are just as many of them, as there are in "The Tribe." The first Sunday in August was their annual family reunion. Everybody who had any connection to the family would descend to this small east Texas town for the weekend.

Back to my crush. I was rendered speechless whenever I'd see him. Time stood still. He was shy, so all he said to me was, "Hello." But that was enough to keep me coming back, year after year, just to see him. It was like in the commercials where the guy and girl are running in slow motion through the fields to meet each other, arms extended, until they meet, and he scooped her into his arms, twirling her around, as they embrace. But in reality, we were in Chandler, Texas on Two Street, in August's 97 degree sun, fighting fire ants and sweating like pigs.

I watched for hours as he played basketball with his cousins, silently cheering for him, as he pulled up on his jump shot. I'd strategically be in his way, as he walked into the house, so he'd have to say excuse me to get by. Sounds desperate, but any words from him were all right by me because he just didn't talk. For three years, I had a crush on him, and never thought once about talking to him. Just seeing him for that weekend was enough for me.

Fast-forward to 1991. We have grown up. Maybe not, we have grown older. We've changed. Or have we?

He had become a commissioned, second lieutenant in the army and was stationed in Oklahoma. A recent college grad, he was in pursuit of law school and maintaining world peace.

I had left east Texas for the bright lights and big city life of the Dallas/Ft.Worth metroplex five years earlier. I had a very good job in the travel industry. I was dating a very sweet guy, Wayne*, who truly cared for me. There had never been any communication with Martin, ever, but Mena, my intelligence implant, would periodically let me know what was going on in his life.

As fate would have it, there was a death in his family, and he went to Chandler for the funeral. Afterward, he went to Mena's house to change his clothes. While they chatted, *he asked about me!* Oh, My God in heaven! This time, my girl Mena, who was on her job, knew that I was still affectionately drawn to her cousin. She picked up the phone and called me while he was there.

The phone rang. I could hear the mischief in her voice, as she playfully asked, "What are you doing?"

"Nothing, just talking to Wayne and watching a movie."

"Take the phone and go to the bathroom for a minute.

*Wayne is a fictitious name; not the real name of the character.

And while I attempted to ask her what she was up to, the voice on the other end of the phone changed and almost made me faint. It was him!

{Press Pause, please} Let's talk about the voice. It was somewhere between baritone and tenor, smooth as velvet, and calming as only a real man could be. And the words he said to me, I'll never forget. "Sweetheart, how are you?" Oh my God, again! It's a twenty-five-year-old version of Denzel Washington talking to me.

I was going to die, right then because he has called me "Sweetheart!" (All along we've been running in the field toward each other....when he called me Sweetheart. We'd finally connected!) I don't remember the next two minutes of the conversation, because I sat there, on my bathroom counter, looking in the mirror at myself, startled.

When I regained my composure and as we made small talk, he asked if I had plans for the evening.

I nervously replied, "Not really."

He asked, "Well, some of us are going out tonight, would you like to meet me at Beamers?"

Never thinking about my boyfriend sitting in my living room, I quickly replied, "Yeah, I'll see ya there around ten." We hung up, and I returned to my living room, looking as proud as I did when I pulled the no school trick on Mama and Daddy. Wayne had to work that evening, and I had made plans to have dinner with my girlfriends. Well, that would change slightly because after dinner we were going to Beamers.

Our movie went off, and Wayne kissed me good-bye. He said, "Have fun tonight; I'll call you tomorrow."

Squeaky and Angela took forever coming to pick me up. We didn't arrive until midnight, but there he stood at the door, still waiting for me. He hadn't changed a bit, just a hint of a mustache on his upper lip, adding age to his otherwise boyish face. Oh, but the face. LL Cool J's dimples landed on Will Smith's face and body, and all of them were within an arm's reach. Could this be it? I believe it could.

My girlfriends laughed at me all night, as I danced with him every time he asked. No other guy stood a chance, as long as he was there. I had my own prince charming for a few hours. As we danced, I noticed his fan club eyeing me down. With a wink of my eye to him, he pulled me closer and we danced. We danced until his EnVogue wannabe fan club left one by one. Their impatience got the best of them. They were smart ladies. They knew this one was mine, and I wasn't letting him go. He had stolen my heart as a child, and finally, I was in his arms. Wayne, who? This was the next General Colin Powell.

With that, the courtship started and we were married. I loved the very air this man breathed. Even when others commented that I was not good enough to marry him, we became husband and wife, for better or for worse, forsaking all others. Everything he did was right in my eyes, and I didn't care who disagreed. I couldn't help but smile every time he came near me. My elbows smiled, my eyelashes smiled, my shoulders smiled. Even my ears grinned whenever he would walk into the room. -If he was wearing his military dress blues, *other parts* of me smiled as well. With every step he would take near me, the cadence of my heartbeat skipped, and only calmed when he'd take me into his perfectly chiseled arms and hold me. He was my "Top Gun" my "Officer and a Gentleman." He said the right things, and held me the right way to always assure me, "Everything is gone be alright, Shortie."

We would have two beautiful daughters who would make the lovely picture complete. Jordan looks exactly like her father would look with ponytails. She also has his quiet, caring demeanor. Jamie is my identical twin. Quick-witted like me, intelligent like me, and a comedienne, like... Both are athletes like their father, but divas in their own right, like their mother. Our lives would be perfect...for a while.

The End. Thank you for buying my book.

Love, Patrice

Not hardly. So now, here we are. You've met me and the major players in my life, my family and some of my friends. Seems like a lot of people, huh? It's only fair to let you know, by the time you reach the end of the book, some of my supportive cast won't be there.

Some were there, when I cried; others were there to make me cry. Others were there to lend support, while some stood in line to borrow money. A few remained in the background, but said enough to rally my spirits during the tough times, when I needed them most. And still others helped me to acknowledge and understand my limitations. Others took a more prominent position to teach me a lesson.

Some hammered out the rough places to discover the hidden soft spots; others rubbed me wrong, and made me callous. Some were there to laugh with me, others to laugh at me. Nonetheless, all were there to shape my life.

Now get your black suit and black dresses ready, we've got funerals to attend. We're leaving the front porch, and going to the front pew at church. It'll be okay. God is in control. But as you will see, despite what life has thrown at me, I choose to be happy. So should you.

Chapter 5 "Losing Jane"

First of four not-so-sweet sips of water...

The television was on in the den, and it was probably around 6:30 in the morning when I heard Mama talking to Daddy. She asked him, "What is Sweet's real name?" From beneath my favorite blanket I mumbled, "Hattie Preston. Why do you want to know?" Sweet and my sister, Jane, were buddies.

I climbed out of my bed and went into our den (in Y2k4 jargon that's the great room) and sat between Mama and Daddy. As I stretched to clear the cobwebs from my mind, I was surprised to see Sissy and Andy, my niece and nephew, sitting in front of me. They looked different. They didn't say anything. They just sat there. Either I was still sleep, or something weird was going on. I had just seen them last night. They had come to Athens with Jane to buy shoes for the prom. *If they went to the prom last night, why are they here at 6:30 am?* Mama put her arm around me and said, "Toody, there was a fire last night, and Jane didn't make it out. She died in it." This couldn't be real. That was the first time I can remember time standing still.

Nawwww, not my big sister. Dead? Couldn't be. She was just here not more than twelve hours ago. This had to be wrong. Jane was just here, yesterday, standing right there by the refrigerator talking about Andy and Sissy's first prom, and how she was going to wait up for them to find out all the details. We went to Penney's to buy Andy's shoes. She talked about her upcoming graduation from nursing school and her recent trip to New Orleans with her class. MY SISTER WAS NOT DEAD! I DIDN'T WANT TO HEAR IT!

But not one tear filled my eyes. Instead, I went back into my dark bedroom and sat. I didn't talk to anyone. I just sat there for a while. At the age of ten, I was about to learn first-hand what it meant to be a family — to have a little bit and share it all, whether it was food, clothing, a house, or even parents. I was about to learn something that none of the prestigious professors of Yale, Harvard nor Oxford could ever teach in a classroom. I was about to learn what it meant for parents to sacrifice for their children.

I was about to live the reality show of a young man — a young black man — growing up without his natural mother, and his father living a three-hour airplane trip away from him. But against all odds, he'd be able to snub his nose at what society would say about black boys who grow up with no father present. Andy would be the one. He would grow up to make all of us proud, and it wouldn't take much for him. Ya know why? It's simple, because we all grew up knowing right from wrong. If, for one moment, Andy had tuned in to the news to learn that black boys growing up without the father in the home were "at risk," the former governors of Texas, George W. Bush and Ann Richards would have never had the services of the best-looking and best-dressed security detail agent on their payrolls. Somebody forgot to tell Andy that he was at risk.

When water was free, there were no "at risk" kids.

At risk of what? Learning more than others? Working harder than others to get where you wanted to go? Yeah, that's what we were — *at risk* of doing and becoming. The worst thing society can do to a kid today is label them. We were children, nothing more, nothing less. We weren't going to do everything right, but we certainly weren't going to do everything wrong, neither.

{Please press PAUSE} Now that water is no longer free, everybody is somehow categorized according to his or her strengths, weaknesses, or economic status. You can't even take a flight and be treated equally without being platinum. Unless you are a cardholder at Brand X grocery store, you pay more for food. Huh? That's one stinky mess! Lord, where is my daddy? {Press PLAY, please}

Long before entering the travel industry, I remember taking my first unaccompanied flight. I headed to Chicago for the Top Teens of America National Convention, as I served as the National Recording Secretary. (Yeah, little old me.) Nonetheless, arriving at DFW Airport excited and anxious, Mama and I nervously waited as the flight announcements were made. Finally, I was allowed to board. She polished my cheeks with kisses, and reminded me to have fun, and to call her as soon as I landed in the Windy City.

I remember waiting in line on the Jetway in the humid June heat. As the line began to move, and I finally entered the aircraft, the flight attendant greeted me and pointed me toward my seat. Evidently, travelers further ahead in the line struggled to get their oversized bags into the luggage compartment, so I stood in first class, patiently waiting. It didn't take me long to notice the luxuriously appointed leather seats flanking me on either side, while the seats in the larger cabin resembled Roger and Dee Thomas' couch from "What's Happening."

To my left was a businessman wearing a navy blue suit, sipping a bloody Mary while I looked on. He was already seated and drinking his way into the friendly skies, while I restlessly passed the time in the aisle. Across the aisle from him was another middle-aged man dressed for golf, who gave me the head-to-toe visual inspection. I guess I passed it, as I was permitted to continue waiting in line. Seated next to him was another man dressed casually, looking out the window, never paying any attention to me or anyone else.

As I continued my survey in mid-1980s first class demographics, I looked around to find someone seated in this exclusive area who resembled me. Could there be one? Just one? To my dismay, there were none. No, I was wrong: there was one black face...yes! There was our representative, finally! The tall handsome brother stood in the aisle, near the entrance to the coach cabin, taking off his jacket. With his starched white shirt, conservative tie, and navy blue slacks, he turned to me and smiled, as he took out his apron and asked if he could help me with my bag. The only black face I saw in first class, that day, was the one who served those who could afford to sit there.

Twenty years later, as a veteran traveler and a premium level flyer of one of the major U.S. carriers, I checked in an hour early at the Orange County airport. I was tired and hungry because I had been up since four o'clock in the morning to make certain I didn't miss my 6:15 a.m. flight home. In two days, I had inspected and evaluated more hotels than I cared to recall and quite frankly, the beauty of the sunsets, and the majestic sounds of the ocean's waves crashing onto the cliffs in Southern California had lost its appeal two evenings prior. I wanted to go home and sleep in my own bed, and eat my own food, without wondering what it was.

Using my elite status, I exercised my upgrade privilege, and waited with the few other travelers on this Dallas/Ft. Worth bound flight. The agent handed my boarding pass to me, and confirmed my preferred window seat. Yes, I had arrived. Someone had finally recognized me for the important person I was. Yeah, right…watch this.

The restaurants would not open until six o'clock, and I longed for something to eat. I approached another gate agent and asked, "Is there breakfast served on this flight?"

"No, you'll only have a beverage," the busy agent replied, quickly peering at me over her rimless bifocals.

"Thanks," I muttered, going back to my seat in the waiting area. *Great, another flight with nothing to eat, except what I've got in my purse, I thought to myself.*

Minutes passed as other guests checked in. One traveler's question, in particular, caught my attention.

"Is there meal service on this flight?"

"Yes ma'am, you'll be served a hot breakfast. You'll get your choice of three items, because you are in the first-class cabin."

I sat straight up, as I wondered, what was the difference between the other traveler and me? Both of us were confirmed in first class, but only one of us would get breakfast? Aww naww, Couldn't be! For a minute, my temper ran hot, and I contemplated stepping out of my Executive Traveler and my Christianity roles for just a moment and step back into my "negritude" to tell her a thing or two. However, I was too tired to fight.

I gathered my briefcase and my purse, went back to the counter with both agents present, and in my most professional, yet tactful vernacular I asked, "Excuse, me. I am confirmed in first class, as the lady seated over there is. When I asked you five minutes ago about breakfast, I was told there was no breakfast served. How then, can she get breakfast, and I can't?"

The previously busy agent looked bewildered. As she looked to her colleagues for help, who offered her none, she stammered "Uhh, umm, you know, ma'am, I guess I was wrong. I thought you were traveling coach. There's no breakfast in the coach cabin, only in first class, this morning."

Again, too exhausted to give her an earful, I stood there for a moment wishing my daddy would come and get her told for me. But I smiled and said, "Times have changed, ma'am, and no longer is the world of business dominated by white men. More specifically, the face and the gender of the first-class traveler have changed."

"Yes ma'am, you are right, and I am truly sorry for making such a general statement to you. I apologize."

Forgiving her was easy, as I would never see her again. However, I'm sure she will always remember me. I boarded the aircraft, ordered and ate my breakfast, and never wrote the letter to her company, which I contemplated doing. Recalling Dr. King's wish, that we be judged by the "content of our character," I think she will always remember how uncomfortable she made herself feel by her poor word choice.

When water was free, only white people flew first class....but not no more! (Okay, okay...not anymore)

Due to Jane's tragic death, at the age of thirty-three, our family was transformed from a family of words to one of actions. Instead of just saying, "I love you," we lived it. Sissy and Andy would no longer be my niece and nephew; instead, they became my sister and brother. (It was too confusing to the rest of the world, how I could have a niece and nephew four and five years older than me. So we just changed our relationship).

Sissy and I shared a bedroom, except when I wanted to sleep with my mama, which was most of the time. I think Sissy liked it like that. That way, she could stay on the phone with her old, ugly boyfriend. He really wasn't ugly, but I could never let her know that I thought Egghead was cute.

My parents were in the middle of remodeling and enlarging our den. So when Jane died, instead of enlarging the tiny room, which we all huddled in to watch television, it was left alone. What was going to originally become a large family room became a bedroom for Andy. Besides, in Daddy's eyes, Andy was a fifteen-year-old young man who needed his space.

Jane's death and Sissy and Andy coming to live with us would teach me about sharing. Remember, up until this point, I had lived the life of an only child. My Christmases were filled with memories of whatever I had wanted, I could expect underneath the modest tree. New clothes, bicycle, stereos, games; everything was always just like I had asked. However, after learning of Jane's death, I never worried about what my future Christmases would be. I just wanted my sister back.

They lost everything in the fire. They had no clothes, shoes, pictures and certainly no mother, but that's okay, I would lend them mine. Thankfully, their younger sister, Rochelle, lived with her paternal grandparents, so all the children were alive. And when the community found out about our family's tragedy, they were there. Not just the residents of north Athens across the tracks, but everyone whose paths had crossed my mom and dad's and my late sister's. Everybody did more than their fair share. Rather than used clothing and shoes, people brought brand new things, with tags still on them.

I have never forgotten that day — March 3, 1978. It served as the beginning of a new life for my immediate family and me. Who could ever imagine what it felt like for a fourteen-year-old girl (freshman) and her fifteen-year-old brother (sophomore) coming home from their first prom to find their home engulfed in blazes? How do you describe the hopeful emotion as the fire chief told them that one person made it out alive? What word best describes the immense horror in finding out that the person who got out safely was the live-in boyfriend, and his dog? Neither deserved to die, but, imagine the despair, as two children stood with other family members in the pre-dawn darkness hours of morning, watching their mother's body being brought in a body bag. They stood together in disbelief, but not without divine hope.

What would they do? What could they do? They would do what any other child would do in that situation; they called their "Big Mama." They knew she'd make it all right because her home was their home.

When water was free, we made room for family, and it was never an inconvenience.

Although my sister's body was burned nearly beyond recognition, we didn't sue anybody. Not the railroad company, which refused to break an idle train on the stopped track, preventing access to the house, nor did we file suit against the city (not Athens, but another east Texas town), as its fire crew stood there with little regard, as Jane burned to death. No, it was worthless. Trillions of dollars would never replace my mother's first born; Andy, Sissy and Rochelle's mother, and Reuben's and my big sister. Although there are still many unanswered questions regarding her death, we don't talk about it much. We resolve that the secret things belong to the Lord and in His appointed time, all truths will be revealed.

I'll prove this to you by the end of the book. Just keep on reading.

***

Chapter

6 "My Brother Reuben"

Second of four bittersweet sips... My Bubba (not to be confused with the redneck variety; there was nothing hillbilly about my brother)

My older brother Reuben, who was twenty-years old when I was born, was the middle child and a boy. That made him my mother's favorite. (At least that's what thought when he would come home.) All he would have to do was pick up the phone and call to announce, "Mother, I'm coming home Sunday." The kitchen would applaud with excitement, as pots and pans would start to fly. It didn't matter what he ordered, she was cooking it — and more. I know she loved him more than me because she knows I hate bananas, and every time his big head would come home, she'd make a banana pudding. Well, I didn't want any of it, anyway. He could have it — he and the monkeys — because that's whom God made the bananas for, not humans.

He never let me live it down that he was the baby for twenty years, and then I showed up. When I was about six years old he told me that I was adopted. He had convinced me that I didn't look like anybody in the family, and that my real family was in Alaska. All the while, he was the only coffee-colored child my mother had, but according to *him*, I didn't look like *them*.

Another time, he told me that because I was a menopause baby, I was retarded, but Mama didn't want to hurt my feelings by telling me. He also told me that cobwebs tasted like cotton candy. When I didn't believe him, he let me climb up on his shoulders, as he took me outside and found some for me to taste. My loving older brother also told me if I took the front of the television off, that the Jackson 5 were actually inside, and they would come out and sing to me. So, I went to the kitchen and got a butter knife and proceeded to hack at getting the front of the TV off, until Mama caught me. Reuben had conveniently left the house when I was busted.

Reuben was a smooth chocolate brother with "good hair," which noticeably made him look a little different from me. He and Jane both had beautiful hair. He served in the Army during the Vietnam War and was discharged with the Purple Heart. Like most veterans of that conflict, he didn't talk much about the experience, but made sure that we all knew he could still shoot an M-16, and would go and find one, if needed. Rube had a great sense of humor, but greater than his sense of humor was his love for his family. From his first marriage he had a daughter just six years younger than me.

When I became an adult, Reuben and I shared a very special relationship, different from most brother/sister relationships, which transcended our ages. Never intrusive into my affairs, he remained just a phone call away, if I needed him. He was the kind of big brother everybody needs. The advice he offered was filled with worldly wisdom, and his own brand of Reuben Arthur humor. Much like his mother, he would tell you the truth, but rather than being stern like Mama, he would put a spin or an example on it that would ensure you'd never forget it.

For instance, in the early 90s when many of the televangelists were being exposed, as the media uncovered their dirty deeds, Reuben's comment on it was, "See, look at that mess. It's gon' be some stuff going on, with them folk tryin' to get to heaven. I can already tell it!" He continued to break it down.

"How you gon' go on TV and tell the public that if you don't get a million dollars you gon' die? I can't wait till we get to heaven. I'm gon' ask the Lord if I can preach my first sermon to them, while they wait outside the pearly gates, trying to strike up a deal."

As he took out his white handkerchief, and proceeded to mock our old preacher back home, he wiped his brow, raised his index finger toward heaven and said, "My text will come from 1Reuben 1:1, and it says, "You can't BS the king!"

With that said, silence halted all conversations for about two seconds because we feared that lightning might strike. It didn't last long because in our hearts, we knew he was right. We'd just never heard it described like that. We couldn't hold back the laughter because he was right on point.

"There's gonna be lots of splaining and begging going on, when a few of them get to the pearly gates," he laughed.

"And I already know I'm getting in because I know the truth: heaven ain't got no cover charge."

My most beautiful story of my brother "Bubba" is the one of his death, and moreover, just how much I love him for what he did for me. Just like my daddy, Reuben died before I finished having my fun with him. He had just remarried and his new bride was expecting their first child. (His third, actually, but it's a long story…maybe in the next free water book.) We were all excited. At the age of forty-eight, they were expecting a child. I constantly reminded him of his "menopause baby" comment he made to me twenty years earlier.

We never knew that it wasn't God's plan for Reuben to ever see his baby. He passed from this life September 30, 1995. Reuben Arthur, II, was born two months later. Once again, without my permission, death snatched someone else from me who I loved, dearly. But unlike when Jane died, I was an adult when Reuben passed and had watched how my mother dealt with death and dying. Daddy died three hundred sixty four days after Jane did. Then my granny passed. Two of Mama's brothers died, as well as the niece who she had adopted and raised as her own. Mama never cried much, and therefore, we never did show very much emotion. She said it wasn't called for. Her speech went something like this: "When someone dies, we have to accept it as God's will, and go on. All the hollering and screaming you do will not bring them back. So don't go in here embarrassing yourselves. We will not go into this funeral disrespecting ourselves or ____ (the deceased). I expect you to cry, but remember, you have to live past this day. If you've treated them right, and loved them the way you should, then you don't have anything to regret. So, we loved _____ and we did our best, so we can walk in here with our heads held high. If it gets too hard for you, think about the good times. You got to remember the good times. You kids got to remember, it's not our will, but God's will that must be done, right?"

Then she'd ask if we understood, and if we were all right. If the answer was no, she'd dig around in her purse for a Xanax, break it in half, and split it between two people. She'd share them with whoever needed them. She'd pass them out like Tic Tacs to ensure that we'd not misbehave. To this day, without the Xanax, we still honor her rule. There's no acting up at a family funeral, just ask anybody. (But I've got news for her, when she dies, I plan to PERFORM! She won't be there to stop me, and there won't be enough ushers in the church to catch me.) It's okay to laugh if you want to...I am laughing, myself.

But back to Reuben. He died of a rare heart disorder, which normally took the lives of its victims within a year. But he fought for four years with it. So, when he was admitted into the hospital for a routine procedure, we thought nothing of it. However, I became alarmed when my husband called me at work, and told me that I needed to call home because Rube was in the hospital. When I talked to Mama she said, "I want you to fly home tomorrow to see your brother." I told her I would. Because I worked in the travel industry, getting a ticket was not a huge deal. Besides, I had her newest gold MasterCard, so it would be *really* easy to do. I didn't hear any great concern in her voice, but I asked to speak to Sissy. Now, you have to understand that Sissy and I have an unspoken understanding between sisters, "Give me the truth, nothing but the truth." When she answered, I didn't ask how she was or how Reuben was; I just went straight to the heart of the matter.

She said, "Hello,"

My immediate question to her was, "Do I need to pack for a funeral?"

She replied, "Girl, naw; just come home," with a reassuring giggle.

To that, I said, "All right, because I don't want any surprises when I get there."

She said, "Everything's okay. Big Mama just wants everybody here."

With that, I booked the flights for Martin, the girls, and me. Thanks to Delta Airlines, we headed for Dallas. Rochelle met us at the airport and drove us to the hospital. I don't remember much about the conversation in the car that day. But I know I was scared, and usually, I'm never afraid. The fear of the unknown had swallowed me. I didn't know what to expect when we got there.

At the hospital, we were ushered into his room, and there he lay…or someone who looked like my brother would look after a train wreck. His face was swollen, his eyes closed and a tube was taped to his nose. His hands were restrained to the rails of the bed, and the wavy hair that I envied was somewhat disheveled because he had been confined to the bed for so long. That was not what I expected, nor was it something that I could handle. I looked at him for a moment and quickly looked away because the sight was more than I could bear. But I could never let him see me cry. I cried because I knew this would be the last day of his life. I knew that we were all sharing in the final hours of his time on earth. I recognized that although he was bound to the bed, I knew that within hours he would be eternally free.

I remember commenting, "He's going to be all right because he's got his football game on." He loved football. It didn't matter who was playing, as long as there was a game on. I knew then that I was simply babbling, but I kissed him on his forehead, and walked out of the ICU area to make room for someone else, and to try and regain my composure.

The children were hungry, and frankly, I didn't like what I was feeling or seeing. I didn't want to be there — waiting for him to die. So at my suggestion, we loaded up the kids and went to get some dinner. I don't remember who all went, I just know we ate and came back on time. As we entered the ICU area, we were met with the P.A. system booming, and nurses running. "CODE BLUE...CODE BLUE...STAT!" I knew it was for my brother. The end had come.

But I was wrong. Thank God! Although while we were at dinner, he had gone into cardiac arrest, they were able to revive him. We again assembled ourselves around his bed, and silently watched and waited. Sissy, who has dabbled in the medical profession (just like her mother and Mama), asked me to step out into the hallway with her. She pointed the heart monitor out to me, and told me to look at his heart rate. And together, we watched as he drifted from this life into eternity. The rate dropped from 56…to 43…to 38…to 21 and that's when we heard those familiar words booming for my brother…"CODE BLUE…CODE BLUE…STAT!!!"

But this time it would be different. We wouldn't get another Fisher High School story, or another wise crack about how much better he looked that the rest of us. This time, this was it. His life on this side of the Jordan River was over.

After the doctors confirmed his death, we went back into his room, and silently stood…and looked. Nothing really needed to be said, so we remained quiet until Andy broke the silence, leading us in prayer. We thanked God for the wonderful life, which had just ended. We wept silently, but accepted God's will. Our family prepared for the void, which no one else could ever fill. The husband, the son, the soldier, the father, the friend, the uncle… all of those people, in one body, died that Saturday evening.

After we left the hospital I learned that Reuben waited for me to get there, before he died. According to Andy, when they told him when my flight landed, and that we were safely on the ground, he nodded his head in acknowledgement. In immense discomfort, he never attempted to say anything; he simply nodded as if to say, "I'll hold on till she gets here." After we made it to the hospital and I had a chance to see him, talk to him, and kiss him…and left for dinner, that's when he decided for himself that it was time to go to heaven. He started to give up on this life and die, but the medical staff intervened, and resuscitated him. When we came back from dinner, he did it again, and this time accomplished his mission. He was ready to go. And when and everybody he loved — his wife, his mother, his daughter, nieces and nephew, and only sister were all there, he made his exit. Could he have known when the nurses were attending to others? Maybe so, maybe not; regardless, he slipped away from us peacefully.

I will always love my brother for holding on until I could get there. *That's love in its purest, most humble form...waiting for his little sister, to arrive before he left to die.* That's all right by me. It's awesome to be loved that much. He put off heaven for a moment, just so I could see him alive.

I was honored when Terri, my sister-in-law, asked that all of our family be involved in the funeral arrangements for him. She didn't have to, but that's just the kind of angel she is. Even though she carried his child, and could have been selfish and wanted everything her way, she, instead, wanted us there every step of the way. She loved my brother, and took care of him in such a way that we remain indebted to her today. She still hasn't remarried, but I hope she does because she deserves someone wonderful. Although, there'll never be another Reuben Arthur.

When we went back to their apartment for the first time, to gather his clothes for burial, Terri, her mother, my niece Tiffany and I all climbed the stairs quietly, thinking our own private thoughts. I thought about the last time Terri had been there; they were there together. I worried that it might be tough on her. After all, she was seven months pregnant. However, upon opening the door to the apartment and walking in, a few minutes passed when she said, "It doesn't hurt like I thought it would." Her mother commented, "That's because this house is so full of love."

That did it for me. I started to cry again because what her mother said was so true. Rube loved everybody, and they loved him in return. It was pretty quiet in the apartment, so she turned on the radio, and like Reuben was speaking through the airwaves, Michael Jackson's timid voice sang, "You are not alone...though we're far apart, you're always in my heart." That was one of the many memorable things to happen to us over the course of the next three days.

We picked out his favorite gray suit, and his trademark scarf he wore around his neck during the fall. This last dance for my brother would definitely be one to remember. So the clothing, the coffin and the service would have to be fitting for the best brother in the world. She asked me to select the casket, and help her to write the obituary. Although it was very special to me, it's an honor that I had never thought I'd have. I chose a black casket, which was very appropriate for what he was wearing, and it furthermore spoke of the classy, elegant brother who would rest peacefully inside.

As we climbed into the van to go meet with the memorial park staff to select a place for burial, the radio was on. As soon as we were all buckled in, Boyz II Men and Mariah Carey's "One Sweet Day" came on. The lyrics echoed, "And I know you're smiling down on me from heaven, like so many friends we've lost along the way, and I know eventually, we'll be together, one sweet day"....second occurrence. More tears from me.

I passed a television set in an office near where we would meet, and just in passing by, suddenly, the program was interrupted with a special report. The newscaster said,

"Ladies and gentlemen, we interrupt this broadcast to let you know that the jury has reached a verdict in the murder case of O.J. Simpson." I thought to myself, *I'm here, grieving for my dead brother, and O.J. Simpson stands on the edge of life in prison. Can't he just go away?* The staff at the cemetery tried their best not to act interested in the bulletin, but I'm sure they were trying to hear it. My brother wouldn't get another chance at life, but even if O.J. got life in jail, he'd get another chance. Not that Reuben died a tragic death, but for a moment, I was angered by the sensationalism of the trial, especially on the day we were tasked with making funeral arrangements. I didn't care if he did it or not. My brother didn't *do it* and had been sentenced to death two days prior. I thought, *Why today?*

Reuben's funeral was one of the most beautiful services I have ever attended. There were almost as many flowers as there were people. Every color in the spectrum and bloom imaginable was represented. I don't know if any mail was delivered that day because it seemed that everyone from the Main Post Office in Dallas was there. I guess after working in the same place for twenty years, and if you're kind of nice to people, you may make a few friends along the way. My big brother was no exception. The sanctuary overflowed with people, who like me, had a warm fondness for this guy. And as I approached his flag-draped coffin for one final glimpse of him, my tears left. I recognized that he was in perfect peace. He had fought the good fight and left nothing for me to cry about because over the past twenty-eight years, my big brother had given me plenty to laugh about and ponder.

Reuben's best friend from high school provided the eulogy, and other classmates spoke of their experiences with my brother. He was quarterback of their high school football team, and an honor graduate as well. One former teammate recalled how Rube would get the ball and pass it to Harold, who would go "barreling his way to the goal line." It was almost like we were at a Fisher High School reunion. All we needed was Mickey Sanders and his band.

Reuben's former wife, who was also his high school sweetheart, and back door neighbor while growing up, is still part of our family. She sat with us, just as we expected her to. Although their marriage failed, our love for her and their love for each other did not. They simply changed the rules of their relationship and their tax filing status to "single," but remained the closest of friends because they had a daughter to think about. She and his new wife enjoy a great relationship, as well. That's the kind of a family we are.

Reuben loved jazz, and by some divine appointment, a saxophonist from one of his favorite spots, who had heard of his passing, came to the service and asked if he could play a solo. My sister-in-law graciously allowed him to, and his rendition of "He Touched Me" brought tears to everyone's eyes in the sanctuary, including his own. While he attempted to play, he would have to stop to wipe his eyes, but continued on, intermittently stopping to dab the flow of tears spiraling down his cheeks. Our hearts sang with him as he played. As the song came to an end, I smiled at him, through my tears, because he had wailed on that horn like he was out of his mind! David Sanborne, Kenny G or Najee could not have played any sweeter. The standing ovation we gave him was not enough, as this man — this unnamed musician — stopped by, played for us, cried with us and left the sanctuary knowing that he had the attention of an audience not just in the sanctuary, but also in the heavens.

It was after the funeral, as we ate the repast that we listened as people came to extend their condolences. Many remarked about the strength of our family during the service. They marveled at how many of us approached the podium to speak about Rube. I spoke, and so did Sissy, his daughter Tiffany, and Mama did as well. They were amazed at how at peace we were, and how well we dealt with our sorrows. Little did they know, that's at the very core of our existence as "The Em's" kids. Strength and integrity (and Xanax) are the marks of her children. Sometimes we slip up, but for the most part, we don't compromise those first two.

I worried about Mama because I suddenly realized that she had outlived two out of three of her children. When I wanted to comfort her, she comforted me. She softly told me, "This is just God's answer to my prayer. Patrice, no mother wants to ever see her child suffer, and I asked God to take away his pain." (I joked to myself thinking, *I hope she never prays for me because when she does, the population changes. She can pray you right off the face of this earth. And I certainly don't want to be child number three that she outlives!)* When I told her it was okay for her to cry, she told me, "It's okay for you to cry, too." So, we had our moment of shared tears and hugs, and we both felt better. That's probably one of the few times I have ever seen my mother cry. But that is probably the first time our hearts really connected at another level. There was something supernatural about that day. The feeling is still difficult to explain.

I knew she was all right, then, but I was worried because at the time I was living in South Carolina. I knew Sissy, Andy and Rochelle were in Texas, and would be checking on her, but I had an innate desire to be closer to my mother, just to know for myself that she was okay. She was fine.

Chapter 7 "My Marriage and the Tender Eyed She Devil"

What does the devil look like? I guess that even as an intelligent and spiritually sound adult, I had maintained the childhood description of the enemy, as the one I learned in Sunday school and saw on Halloween. You know the one. He wears a red suit, has a tail, and horns and holds a pitchfork in his hand. That devil, remember him?

After a few buckets of tears and a countless number of heartbreaks, I am now relieved to know that to a mature Christian, the devil looks nothing like that. On the contrary, the devil looks most like the things that you and I secretly crave and almost obsess over. For some, he may be the gentle mahogany-hued brother, with the charming voice, whose words could swoon you right out of your clothes. For others, the devil may be the woman clad in the painted on red leather pants, with the "video girl" body, driving the candy apple red convertible Corvette, with the personalized license plate that reads, "DAN G RUS". {Press PAUSE}Why would anyone in their right mind want someone who has already labeled *herself* dangerous? {Press PLAY}

Others may mistake their insatiable desire for money, for everything but the enemy. From 1 Timothy 6:10, we already know "the love of money is the root of all evil." Some have found the devil to be in the adrenalin rush received after closing a multimillion-dollar deal. Whatever the case, too much of a good thing can be unhealthy (and I am not just referring to sweets). King Solomon taught us that, right? How many hundreds of women (wives and concubines) did he have before he died having never reached his sixtieth birthday?

For whatever reason, the enemy found my husband, and this time she looked a lot like me. She was about my height and weight. She, too, had long hair (but hers lacked the black cotton candy consistency of mine, as she was part Asian). Her ethnicity did not matter to me. Her dirty deeds did; however. She, like me, found my husband extremely attractive. But where my vision is 20/20 uncorrected, and I can see straight, hers tended to cross a bit, thus helping me to coin my satirical nickname for her, "The Tender Eyed She Devil."

It is my assumption that not only was her vision crooked, but her motives matched her flawed vision. What my husband did as a gesture of kindness toward her, she misunderstood, magnified, twisted and turned, until she had made her way into our household.

Martin witnessed an auto accident, where someone hit her car and failed to stop and render aid. He, the greatest Boy Scout, pulled over to see if she was all right and offered to let her use his cell phone to contact the police. He stayed there with her until the authorities arrived. Then he came home to tell me all about what happened. This story, though amusing, was not out of the ordinary for him because he would always extend himself to help anyone in need. That was just his nature. He'd give good money to the pan handlers begging on the street corners, pick up hitchhikers, and bag our groceries at the store so the bag boys wouldn't have to get wet if it was raining. (Hello! That was *their job*?) Anyway, he was just always available to help anyone in need. However, the Good Samaritan gesture set the stage, and began destroying what was once a wonderful marital relationship, a picture perfect family, and ultimately, the world of two wonderful little girls.

I am certain that it was her bad vision that prevented her from seeing the gold band on the third finger of my husband's left hand, which I had placed there four years earlier at our wedding. On the other hand, it could have been the very thing that attracted her. She was probably one of many women who operate under the concept "There's nothing like a good challenge." Or maybe, she was smitten by his perfect smile, or the certain savior faire of my pork and bean eating Kappa Man. I don't know exactly what it was, but she felt she had to have him. She chased him all the way to his grave.

I couldn't help but see the evil in her, the sneaky little imp. But when I cautioned my husband about her, he let me know how wrong I was, and that it seemed I was a bit jealous.

Based on the characteristics she showed me during those years of embarrassing pain, I can't help but to see the gross resemblance between her and the evil one. Scripture tells us that in the Garden of Eden, the serpent was more subtle than *any* beast of the field, which the Lord God made. (Genesis 3:1) This very description of the devil almost spelled out her name to me. Slithering, slick and slimy; all of these rather non-flattering adjectives convey my thoughts about how I felt about this woman.

If any credit is to be given to her, it may be that I should applaud her efforts. She had devised a plan, and diligently worked her plan; however, she just didn't plan for the object of *our* affection to *die*.

She was quite clever in her approach, and found it harmless to dedicate a love song to him on the local radio station. The ironic timing of her little stunt was almost perfect. He had just picked me up from work to have lunch with him. As usual he opened the door for me and said, "You gotsta pay me." That was his way of making sure that I kissed him before we ever went anywhere.

The radio was on and we casually chatted en route to our favorite little Chinese restaurant. As we pulled in to the parking space, the disc jockey introduced the next song, with a dedication whose words still resonate in my ears, "This one goes out to the fine Kappa Captain driving the MX6 at ….." My jaw dropped as I looked over at him to see what he thought about this misplaced display of misguided affection. Apparently, he was caught off guard as much as I was that she would do such a thing. He squirmed as he tried to explain that he didn't know the woman, and that he had no idea what she was up to. Feeling hopeless and embarrassed, I was yet passively thankful that we weren't in a car full of people, who would have heard it, too. I accepted what he said, but didn't say a word through the entire meal. It never dawned on me that the rest of Columbia, South Carolina's R&B listeners heard it too, including my co-workers. I hoped that they hadn't heard it, but upon returning to my desk, the assistant manager looked at me and asked, "Patrice, isn't Martin a Kappa?" She knew, but she was messy, too.

Her next clever deed happened about a week later. While I was at home doing laundry, the phone rang. On the other end was my loving husband, who called me from his office, with excitement and uncontrollable delight in his voice to tell me, "Honey, I got the roses you sent me. They're beautiful."

I replied, "You did?"

He answered, "Yeah, I did. You are too much. I didn't expect them today. It's not my birthday or anything."

I said, "That's interesting because I didn't send you any flowers today."

{Press PAUSE} It was customary that I would send him flowers or occasionally have a pizza delivered to his office for no apparent reason, other than my sincere love for him. So rightfully, he was sure that I had done it this time. Once again, he was wrong and didn't know what to say or do. She succeeded in making him look like a fool once again. The score was now, The Devil 20, Our Marriage -20. {Press PLAY}

"Bring them d*** flowers home to me! I'm calling the florist to see who sent them."

"No, no, don't worry about it, I'll take care of it, and return them to the florist, myself."

"Nawww, I said bring 'em home with you. I want to know who sent them!"

"Sweetheart, there's no need for you to get any more upset. I'll take care of it. I promise."

I would have gladly informed her in no uncertain terms what she could do with her roses. I don't know what steps he took, but by the time he made it home, the flowers had disappeared.

At that time, he was still unaware of how she found him on the Army's largest training facility in the world. But remember, the devil is sneaky and subtle. All she needed was the challenge. Not only did she find his office address and phone number, but also she managed to find our home phone number, and later on his parent's home number. Imagine that.

{Press PAUSE, again} Now, let's get something perfectly understood between you and me; just because I'm a saved woman, doesn't make me a stupid woman. I haven't been saved all of my life. There was a more foolish time in my life, when I played this same game, too. So I was well aware of what she was trying to do. Her game was weak because when I played the same devilish game, the wife didn't find out. *I don't think…or did she?* {Press PLAY} Once again, could it be that my mother knew what she was talking about when she always said, "What comes around goes around…the way you get a man may be the way you lose a man."

Now, since you and I are having a casual conversation from the comfort and safety of my mother's front porch, I'll let you in on something. I know that the *she-devil* didn't get all of that information by herself. She had some help, and I think it was from the one whom I loved so dearly — the one I esteemed above all others. I'll never accuse him, but I've got a feeling that's where the leak came from.

Christmas Eve 1997, all of Martin's family made the trip to Kansas for the holiday celebration. His mother had dressed the house in festive red, green and gold. Bulbs, balls and ribbons adorned the walls. The biggest Christmas tree I've ever seen dominated the family room, as did the bounty of gifts flowing beneath its branches. Twinkling lights, glowing ornaments and artificial icicles teased the children, as they anxiously awaited Santa's arrival. Hanging over the fireplace in the hall were personalized stockings for each of Big Mama and Big Daddy's eight grandchildren.

We gave life to the lyrics of Nat King Cole's "The Christmas Song." Only, we didn't have the chestnuts, but Big Daddy always had plenty of peanuts and pecans. For those who would dare try it, "doctored up" egg nog chilled in the refrigerator. The warm scents of vanilla and nutmeg sweetened the air, as two sweet potato pies browned in the oven. Growing anxious, in anticipation of the pies and Santa, I employed our oldest nephew to make an ice cream cone for me, and I would pay him twenty-five cents. The rest of the family followed my lead, and before going to bed that night, we counted his earnings for the evening. It was a pretty lucrative temporary assignment for a thirteen-year-old. Although the weather outside was cold enough for snow, the warmth in the house radiated from the joy of the holiday, and family love; not from the crackling fire in the fireplace.

While I helped my mother-in-law in the kitchen, the telephone rang.

"Trece," she said, "Answer that for me, Baby, while I get the pies."

"Hello."

The whiny, high-pitched voice on the other end asked, "May I please speak to Martin?"

"Sure, may I tell him who's calling?"

She snickered and said, "This is __________" Her guilty giggle conveyed her pleasure in letting me know who was calling.

I personally handed the cordless phone to my husband, who had come into the kitchen to throw something away. With the look of hatred in my eyes, he realized something was wrong. I felt like dying. Was no place sacred from this witch? There we were, in the sanctity of his parents' home, with his brother and sisters and all the children, seemingly enjoying "the most beautiful time of the year"... and she called. She showed no remorse and apparently felt no disrespect in calling either. Women like that rarely do.

This time, with tears in my eyes, I walked away from where everyone was gathered. As he finished his telephone call, I sat alone in the darkness of his childhood bedroom, fuming! It's enough that she stalked him while we were at home, but to track us down half-way across the country was a little more than I could tolerate. I was embarrassed beyond mention. I wondered if his family had condoned his dirty dealings with her, while I stood there looking like a fool. I never confronted them about it because I didn't want to know the truth. My trust for his family began to fade as the reigns of my marriage slowly slipped away. I silently vowed never to return to his parents' home again.

Within minutes, he came into the room, leaving the lights off while offering no apology. Instead, he attempted to explain that he had no idea how she got the phone number. All I asked him was to take me back to Texas to my mother and my family. I knew "dirty girl" didn't have my family's number, too. (I hoped.)

Our fifth wedding anniversary dinner will always remind me of how poor word choice and timing can wreck the greatest intentions. I made reservations at a trendy dinner club in Columbia, while he secured a baby sitter for the girls. Upon arriving at the restaurant, we were seated in a quiet corner at a candlelit table for two, just like in the movies. We shared a split of champagne, and as he raised his glass to me, he said, "It's been five years and I knew we would make it. I'm glad I didn't take _______'s advice, when she told me to just divorce you."

This man was my Jesus. *I knew exactly what the Bible says about making an idol and idolatry.* But that didn't apply to me. Idolators were those people who worshipped things like cars and jobs. I wasn't one of *those* people. I attended church regularly and was fully aware about how God feels about having no other gods before him. I just loved my husband. He was my everything. I stopped tithing at church because he didn't trust most ministers, but found his joy in helping others himself. I put his needs, goals and desires above my own. That's why I didn't mind the day when he mentioned wanting to go forward with starting law school. I thought to myself, *One promise I didn't fulfill to my daddy might happen through my husband. Our "Lake Athens Career day conversation" could still happen.* I was happy for him, although it meant finishing my undergraduate degree would be put off for a while.

When he wanted to help out family members financially, I agreed because that's what we were supposed to do. (According to whom, I don't know; but that's what I thought.) When he encouraged me to quit my day job to open our own family business; which was absolutely absurd and against my better judgment, I did it. I did it to please him. I was never the entrepreneurial type, but he wanted me to run my own business. That was his dream for me, not my own. I lived it out, as best as I could…disappointed and angry most of the time. After many tries, prayers and tears, it took me another three years to figure out the calling on my life is not in administration, but in support.

If you ever saw the mistreated black woman's battle cry, *"Waiting to Exhale,"* I was Angela Bassett's character, Bernadine, as she learned of her husband's infidelity with the other woman. I felt her pain, as their seemingly perfect lives revealed a pretense only to distract the onlookers. Our lives truly resembled each other's. Although she was a fictional character; I was living out her story in real life. (No, I didn't win $900,000 in the divorce, but stay tuned; the story gets interesting.)

Fast-forward one more year to 1998. From June to August a sense of prevalent foreboding clouded our home. It was another hot summer evening, and I had come home zonked from a trying day at the travel agency. I wasn't making enough money, but I was attending every "grip and grin" luncheon the Black Chamber of Commerce sponsored. If I had to eat one more chicken breast hidden under a thick, yellow gravy and another long stemmed, undercooked green bean, I would surely turn into one of them. Mentally, I was exhausted and emotionally, I knew something was wrong, but I just couldn't put my finger on it. Physically, I was zonked.

Resting my weary bones on the loveseat, I looked up at him and asked, "Honey, is everything okay? You seem distant."

"Why would you say that, Sweetheart? I'm fine."

"Is there something wrong with you?" he continued.

Joining me on the loveseat, with outstretched arms and a hug, his words soothed the illegitimate discomfort I led myself to believe I was feeling. But in my heart, I knew something was wrong. I believed him until the cell phone bill, which was in my name arrived. It started to tell the tale of what my apprehensions were already telling me. There had been communication between someone in my house to a phone number in South Carolina, and it was not me, nor my daughters.

A few days later, the kids and I came home, and as I entered through the garage door, my girlfriend Tracy knocked at the front door. Rushing to answer the door, and the simultaneously ringing telephone, I missed the call. I opened the door for Tracy and her kids, and invited them in. As our kids got settled and ran upstairs to play, I checked my caller ID and found that the South Carolina phone number had just called my house. Tracy looked at me and I looked right back at her without so much as blinking an eye, as I told her who it was. {Please press PAUSE} This is my childhood girlfriend, and she's got my back. So she's ready for battle. {Press PLAY}

Tracy put her purse down and joined me at the coffee table and said, "Oh yeah, let's call her back, and find out exactly what she needed."

I probably shouldn't have, but I did, because the wife in me wanted to know. After these years, I had to know for myself, what her infatuation with him was. So, I did the wife thing. I dialed the number, nervous and unprepared for what I would learn.

As soon as she answered, she immediately put me on hold, not knowing Tracy was listening. But, just like me, she had a girlfriend, too, who could verify her story. So, there we were, all four of us on the phone, when she began to talk. She said, "It's time you know the truth about my relationship with *your* husband." I listened. She spoke very disdainfully about me...to me. I didn't cry. I didn't argue. In fact, I didn't say a word. I simply listened. I let her tell me what she felt that I needed to know. When she finished *sharing,* she offered to FedEx audio tapes of their most recent conversations to me. I declined. I remembered the Diva's rule number one: *Never let them see you sweat.*

What was this about? Another Monica Lewinsky? If she was only his friend, why would she take the extra step to record their conversations? Could it be that she was intent on blackmailing him?

At the conclusion of the call, Tracy asked, "So what do you think?"

I responded, "I just don't know."

"Are you okay?"

I answered, "Yeah, but my adrenalin flow is so high right now, that I want to run." (Please remember, I have no athleticism in my body.)

She stayed with me for a few hours, but insisted that I come home with her and the kids that night, but I assured her that I was okay. She made me promise that if things got bad for me that I would come to her place. I promised.

That evening, I cooked dinner for my kids and began to cry, as I replayed the conversation with Nasty Nita in my mind over and over again.

The conversation, the cell phone bill, the radio station stunt, and now the audio tapes. With all of the evidence I had, what would I do with it? Now what?

I called his brother to talk to him about it, and just like I thought, he didn't believe any of it. Why did I think he would? For that matter, I didn't even believe it. I didn't want to believe it. Nobody would ever believe what had just happened, except Tracy because she heard it for herself.

Here's what did *not* happen. She never confirmed any intimate contact between them; but she knew enough of *my* business to make me uncomfortable. Events that required that he traveled, she knew of with great detail. Even though I was his personal travel agent, she was his personal assistant. She knew flight arrival and departure times, hotel confirmation numbers, addresses, phone numbers and even room numbers. She spoke about meeting friends he and I had become acquainted with during our time in Arizona. According to her, she was often there with him, while he talked to me on the phone. I never sought to verify any of the information because she had said and done enough. What could I do? What could I say? Nothing.

The confrontation was pretty low key, and considering the myriad emotions that engulfed my mind, it was rather drama free. That is, if you call emotional outbursts, guilty tears and splashing water, drama free.

The next morning, as I sat in a lukewarm bathtub of disintegrating bubbles, psychologically, I was miles away. As they melted away, I was reminded of my failing marriage. It was a bunch of pretty and sweet-smelling fluff, losing the substance to support itself. Love, honesty and trust fizzled away. I was still puzzled about all that I had learned, just hours beforehand.

I could hear the hesitation of his footsteps on the staircase drawing nearer to the guest bathroom. He knew I was in there, but getting in would not be easy. Nevertheless, when he tried to open the door, it simply jiggled. "What was he thinking? That I'd leave the door unlocked for him?" This time, he had lost the privilege of open access to me. Like strangers outside our house, he, too would have to knock to enter any place I was. "Can I come in?" he muttered.

Without answering him, I carefully stepped out of the tub, onto the rug, making certain not to drip water onto the slippery tile floor, and I unlocked the door for him. I was careful to turn around and quickly get back into the tub without making a watery mess on the floor, and certainly without giving him an unsolicited and undeserved peep show. The door opened.

While entering the bathroom, he never looked at me. Ashamed? Shocked? Embarrassed? Guilty? Or was he as angry at me, as I was at him? I didn't care!

As he approached the tub, my mind drifted back to all of the "Nothing's wrong, baby" watered down sorry excuses for guilt I had been fed all those months. The thoughts sparked the tinder box smoldering in my chest. Soon, the internal smoke ignited an unforgivable flame, which burned at the very core of my love and trust for him. The closer he came to me, the hotter the inferno raged, and the further I wanted him away from my heart. The temperate water where I sat seemed to emit an invisible steam, the longer I sat there. Just like the pressure cooker Mama always cooked tough meats in, I was about to blow! There was no room for explanations, no sorrow for his guilt, and no remorse for his regrets. He didn't stand a chance; there was nothing more to say. She had spoken for him.

While he struggled to find the words to utter his heartfelt confessions, in my mind I cursed him out. I silently thought to myself, *Are you apologizing for the relentless pain you've cause me? Or are you apologizing because your silly whore blew your cover? Or are you regretting being caught because your game wasn't as buttery smooth as you thought it was?*

No, I was wrong. He was very remorseful and humble as he made attempts to apologize to me, while never finding the courage to look at me. Sitting on the floor next to the tub, he cupped his face in his hands, and as tears washed his face, he quietly sobbed, "Baby, I'm sorry. All of this stuff started from a *simple lie*."

And there she blows! I interrupted, screaming like a banshee, "Just what the hell is a simple lie? You don't know what a simple lie is and I don't either because there's nothing simple about a lie."

A monsoon of tears streamed through the cracks in his fingers, as he sat there taking my verbal assault like a true soldier, yet still trying to find the right words to say. They never came because they didn't exist. Nothing he could have ever said would have fixed the problem. Every word he spoke reminded me of *her* roses, *her* song dedication, *her* Christmas call to his parents' home, and *her* "just divorce her" comment. No matter what he would have said, I cut him off.

Then I stopped. -And while reaching for a towel to dry myself off, I stepped over him, not caring that I splashed nearly a gallon of water on him, as I continued my rampage. For the first time since I fell in love with him on a hot August afternoon fifteen years past, I deplored him. Since being swept off my feet as an adult, some seven years earlier, this time, I felt swept under the rug. This time, I didn't care about how he felt. Wet, whipped, wicked, coy and clever, caught, trifling, tripped up, troubled...I didn't care. It was my heart that ached. Not his.

While whisking the water from my legs, I quickly cautioned him, "Before you say another word, I want you to know that your nasty little friend called me last night, and sang like a bird."

In a subdued, yet regarded tone, he replied, "I know. She called me after she talked to you and we talked about it."

{Please press PAUSE} Okay...I was thinking, *You thoughtless coward! You've known all night long what this heffa has done to me, and it never dawned on you to call and check on me?* {Press PLAY}

I couldn't get out of the bathroom quick enough. Once again, I felt like running. Lunging for the door, his towering six foot stature and long athletic arms reached over me to impede my attempt at opening the door to leave. Placing himself between me and the door, he made a futile try at hugging me. He missed. With smooth grace that would rival the moves of Muhammad Ali, I ducked beneath his reach, so as not to even allow his flawlessly chiseled body to touch my body, anywhere.

As I tried to leave again, he succeeded in wrapping his once-upon-a-time loving arms around me. The same arms that, in times before, had protected me, comforted me, and held me when I needed him most. This time, they felt like painful pounds of somebody else's insincere flesh enveloping me. They didn't feel the same; and they didn't smell the same because they weren't the same. Those arms had hugged the filthy garbage of another woman, and I couldn't stand the stench.

My demeanor confused him because he had never seen me treat anyone so coldly. Although he had seen me "go off" on friends and family before, I had never been so animated and angry with anything he had ever said or done. Remember, he could do no wrong in my eyes, until now. He knew I was grossly affected by all that had transpired and with all the love in his heart, he pleaded with me. "What do you want me to do? Whatever it takes, I'll do it," he said, still clinging to my partially dried off body, but, never looking at me. His tears streamed down my naked back.

Still steaming and definitely not in the mood to be touched, let alone hugged by the garbage man, I made my needs known to him. It's almost like I called his bluff. "Here's what I *need* you to do," I yelled. "You *need* to pick up the phone and call her to tell her that the relationship is finished. You *need* to tell her, with me on the phone, never to call here again. Finally, I yelled, "This is not what I want, it's what I *need*!"

A puzzling scowl overtook his somber face, as he paused, but quietly resisted, "That's childish, Patrice, and I'm not 'going there' with you."

Refraining from choking him was the best thing I did that day. At that point, I then understood that his friendship, courtship, "whatevership" with her was not worth his honoring my immature request. The indissoluble vows didn't matter anymore; they were now soluble. It stung like a wasp, at the most vulnerable depths of my heart, but enough was said. No longer did I try to make sense of any of the madness. Never again did he attempt to apologize; consequently, never again did I ask for anything else from him. Immediately, I moved out of our bedroom and into the guest room upstairs. Seldom did he receive anything hot from me, not a meal or romance.

He was no longer exclusively mine. Although I had shared my entire life, heart and soul with him, I refused to share him with another woman. This man — the one man to whom I had given my everything — declined to give me the one thing *I needed* in order to keep our marriage in tact. Although he made valiant attempts to appease me with nice dinners, dates, flowers and even a bicycle for our anniversary, it was nothing to me. He offered things, when I needed actions.

When a conversation escalated into an argument later, which resulted in his saying "You should be over it by now," I knew he'd never understand my perspective. It had only been a few months, and he had carried on his rendezvous with her for nearly five years. Against the direction of our pastor, I filed for divorce. I was uncertain about my future because until that very minute, he had been my yesterday, today and tomorrow.

However, I was assured that the children would be fine because I knew, by his admission, that he loved them more than he loved me or anyone or anything else. Or did he?

He expected me to let it go; after he had kept an unauthorized friendship with this woman, I was just supposed to "get over it?" Negro Please!

Chapter 8 "The Best of the Worst Christmas Ever"

The third sip of bittersweet water...

By now, you've seen that every man I've ever loved has died before I could finish loving him. Here's another one.

It was close to noon on Christmas Day 2000, and I had just arrived in Tyler at Sissy's house for our family's dinner. They all complained because I was the last person to make it there, and they didn't understand that the Sock-It-To-Me cake that I had made was not quite cooled, and it would be disastrous for me to drive with a hot cake in the car. Furthermore, the weather was dreadful. Weather alerts flashed across the television screens all morning, discouraging driving given the black ice frozen on highways and overpasses.

Martin and the children had left the house at 5:00 a.m., earlier that morning to drive to Kansas to his family's gathering. Despite his pleasant persistence, I told him and the girls to make this one a "Dad and Daughter Outing," and I'd certainly take the next trip with them. (Doubting that I'd ever go back to Kansas, after the last Christmas I had there.)

It was almost spooky how just two weeks prior, to the date, we had finalized our divorce, and the proceedings were pleasant. I made no demands. We shared custody. He gave me the house. In the midst of it all, we had lunch after the hearing, and committed ourselves to a healthy relationship for the sake of our children. He had come home on Christmas Eve, and it was just like nothing had changed because emotionally, we still loved each other, but could not work past the pride that had devoured us both. I was too angry at him, and like others I know, I was more concerned about how badly he hurt me, to reflect on what I could have done to ease the pain. Nonetheless, we were now divorced.

Martin came into the house, and walked straight into the kitchen to cash in on the holiday bounty, which awaited him there. Smothered chicken, my "ghetto fabulous beans," corn on the cob, potato salad and apple pies crowded the small plate in his hands. He fixed his first plate, and returned to the living room to take off his shoes, as he always did, and drag his socked feet across the carpet, as though to scratch them. He knew just how much that annoyed me…so he did it, and laughed while doing it. The room tingled with excitement, and the children's faces silently expressed their delight in having their parents together. We honored our promise of friendship, in our first holiday as divorcees. They knew that no matter what, we'd be a family, forever.

We watched a movie, and after the girls had fallen asleep, Martin and I plotted our timing for the "Santa Clause Staging" at around 2:00 a.m. I woke him up at 2:20 and we moved the kids into our bedroom as we brought in their toys from the garage. After setting up everything, we hugged each other, and he thanked me for making this Christmas easy for us. He had not been able to purchase all the things for the girls that he wanted them to have, but I picked up the slack, and labeled all the gifts, "From Dad and Mom." He noticed it, and thanked me again for always "being a trooper."

Awkwardly I felt comfortable in his arms, as he again apologized to me for his role in all that had brought our fairy tale to an end. Through my tears, I too, apologized and pledged my support to him as a friend for life. As he gently pushed me away from his embrace, so he could look into my eyes, his words touched my heart, and at the same time startled me.

"I'll be going to Kuwait in January, and will be there for about three months. When I get back home, do you think we could get counseling, and I can come back home where I should be?"

He really caught me off guard, as I stared at him, to make certain that he was saying what I thought he was. My slow reply was, "Do you realize what you just asked me?"

"Yeah, goofy, I know."

"Well, you take care of the army business, and when you get back, if you still feel the same way, we'll talk about it then."

"Just tell me, Patrice. Would it make it better if I ended all communication with her?" he asked, referring to The Tender Eyed She Devil.

"Martin," I interrupted, "the last time you talked about..."

"This is not then. This is now, and if it weren't 3 o'clock in the morning, I'd call her now. But when I get to Mom and Dad's, after I call you to let you know we've made it, that'll be the next phone call I make."

Teasing him, I asked, "So you're putting me in before her?"

He grinned, "You've always been first. Here, I've bought you something for Christmas, but I know you're not going to like it."

We laughed because he always struggled with what to get me on special occasions. He handed me a legal envelope. I thought he was trying to be funny and was giving me his copy of our final divorce decree. But again, I was wrong.

"You know I'm going to Kuwait next month, and anything can happen over there. If something happens to me, the girls will be taken care of, but this is for you."

For years, we kept a crude joke going between us, and he laughed as he repeated it, "If anything happens to me, cremate me, and ride my ashes around in the glove compartment of your new Jaguar."

I opened the envelope and there inside was a $100,000 life insurance policy on him, made out to me.

Ten hours later…

Mena walked into Sissy's house, and rather than come into the living room, where we all were, she turned left and went into the bedroom. Normally, she always makes her entrance known with a nasally signature soprano, "Hey y'all!" But not this time. Shortly after putting her purse on Sissy's dresser, she came into the living room, saying nothing with her mouth, but with her face, she told a story that none of us could believe. Sitting down next to me on the sofa, she gently patted me on my right leg, and said, "I've got something to tell you." I ALREADY KNEW WHAT SHE WAS ABOUT TO SAY. I DON'T KNOW HOW BUT I ALREADY KNEW…

She calmly said, "There's been an accident."

I replied, "Umm hummm."

"Your kids are okay, but they are in the hospital," and before she could complete her next words, I interrupted, "And Martin is dead, huh?"

She replied, "Yeah, he's dead. He lost control of the truck and went into a skid across the median and into oncoming traffic. He was killed instantly when another SUV hit him broadsided, near Stillwater, Oklahoma."

I don't remember what happened for the next few seconds. I just vaguely recall everything moving in slow motion for a minute or two. I remember sitting there momentarily, and then jumping to my feet saying, "I'm all right, but I've gotta get to my kids." I started to gather my things, my purse, my jacket and my car keys. It was time to go!

Mena explained to me that the girls had been critically injured and were in intensive care in Stillwater, Oklahoma. Jamie's arm was fractured, her ankle was twisted and her bladder was crushed. Although I didn't know it at the time, she also had a concussion. Jordan's clavicle was broken, heart was bruised, lungs were bruised and she was being observed for head trauma and kidney distress. While I appreciated what she was telling me, I needed to get to my children. Then the thought of Martin's family hit me like a ton of lead. How were they?

I walked away from the crowds for a minute into another room and got on my knees. In the darkness, I began to sob. *How could this be?* Another Christmas, sitting alone in a dark room, wondering why love has to hurt so bad. Wondering why on this day was death again jacking with my family. I thought about how although we were divorced, I still loved him. How we had just talked about working on a reconciliation, and I had really forgiven him. I recalled every hour we spent together not twelve hours before. The unfair questions battled my reasoning and only life would answer them for me. *Was I really that mad at him? Was it really that difficult to get over the other woman? Now, that he was dead, who would help me to raise these children?*

Silent moments of regret crept into my mind, as I realized just how powerless I was against all of the prevailing circumstances. Someone opened the door and came in to sit with me on the floor. Others joined us. They talked to me, but to this day, I have no idea what any of them said. I only remember; however, the phone ringing, and me getting up from the floor. I again said to everyone, "I'm all right. I'm going to be fine. I've just gotta go."

The attending physician called to let me know about the children's condition. As I listened, her prognosis sounded reassuring, but nothing could replace me getting to my children. I needed to see them. As their mother, only I knew what they looked like when they were all right. I just needed to look at them.

Jamie was awake and the doctor put the phone up to her ear, so that I could talk to her.

"Mommy?" she strained.

Yes, Baby, it's Mommy. How are you, Sweetie?"

"Mommy, where's Daddy? We've been in here a long time and he hasn't come to check on us."

I quickly answered, "Daddy is at another place. He was hurt really badly, but I'll be there when you wake up tomorrow, okay?"

She replied, "Okay, but Jordie is hurt bad."

I encouraged her, "All right, I need for you to be a big girl for me, and do what the doctors tell you to, okay? As soon as I can get on a plane, I'll be there."

"Okay, Mommy. I love you," her voice whispered.

The doctor, hearing the end of our conversation took the phone, explained that she was having problems reviving Jordan, and keeping her alert. She asked for my permission to put Jamie's bed near her bed, and have Jamie talk to her. Of course I agreed, and asked that she let me talk to her once more. When I explained to Jamie what we needed her to do, she said she would do it. I knew she would.

Getting to Oklahoma was an understatement. I had to get there, immediately. I had fourteen years vested in the travel industry, and I knew all the tricks of the trade to get airline tickets, so I was ready. (Besides, I had my mama, and all of her platinum credit cards. We only needed a confirmation number to get us there.) So I thought.

I called the airlines. American, Delta, and Southwest, and all of them told me the same thing. "Due to weather problems in and around Oklahoma, both Oklahoma City and Tulsa airports are closed and will not be opened until tomorrow." In despair, I called Amtrak, and learned that it would have taken me eleven hours to get there by rail. Me? Take an eleven-hour train ride for a thirty minute flight? Never! That was totally out of the question.

My next step was to call one of the local hospitals and charter a helicopter to fly me to Oklahoma. One quoted the cost of $2,500 with insurance; however; both hospitals in Tyler said the same thing that the airlines had previously told me.

We called Andy to let him know what was going on, and to see if he could get an escort from the Texas State Troopers to help us get to Oklahoma. After all, before going to work for the governor, that's what he did. So, he checked on it for me, and interstate 35 north was closed due to the dangerous conditions.

Okay. Down to my last option, I decided to call the army and see what they could do to help us. Yeah, I notified the army of his death. Instead of them showing up at our door with the police, I contacted them. And still, there was nothing they could do for me, given the weather conditions. Totally oblivious to the tragic weather that had just destroyed my family; I remained determined to get to the girls. I was desperate.

I've had an argument with God, once. I yelled at Him, and He said nothing, until I shut up. Here's how it happened. Frustrated, scared, saddened and anxious, I got up from the sofa, and paced around Sissy's coffee table a couple of times. Then I walked into the kitchen, as though God was standing in there in human flesh. Just like He was a man, I stood toe-to-toe with Him and started yelling at Him. I know everybody in the house thought, "Okay, she's lost it, she's talking to the air."

But I stood there and with my hand on my hip and the other hand working. I verbally told God, "I don't like what you just did. I didn't have anything to do with that, and I don't appreciate you letting that happen. I can't get to my kids and Martin is dead, and the roads are closed. What's up with that, God? How you gon' do *me* like this? I'm not doing anything. I can't do anything! I've got enough money to get the airline tickets, but you've got the airports and the roads closed, and I can't do anything. So, here's what I'm going to do, I'm going back to the living room, and I'm going to sit down, and wait for you to do something."

With that said, I did just what I had told Him I would. Returning to the sofa, I sat back down, and didn't say a word. That's when He started speaking to my heart. He told me that was all he had wanted me to do all of my life — just sit down and be quiet, for once. Turn it over to him, so that he could let me see how he had worked out the details, *without my help*. He was tired of competing with me for the glory. Although he allowed me a few "glorious" moments, I had stolen his glory with my "make it happen" attitude. He told me to close my mouth. I did. He told me to be still and wait. I did. He told me when I tell you to move, you do it. I did.

In obedience, I told my mother. "We're not going anywhere tonight. The roads are too bad and the hospital has this telephone number to reach us. Besides, Jordan is still not doing well, so let's just wait here, and maybe get a fresh start tomorrow."

For those who don't know how quickly God responds to and rewards our obedience, this next paragraph is for you. As soon as I acted in obedience, and told Mama our plans for the night, the phone rang again. It was the hospital calling to let me know that with Jamie's (and God's) help, Jordan was now conscious. The doctor said that Jamie persisted telling her sister, "Jordie, wake up...Jordie, you've got to wake up. Get up Jordie!" This all happened within twenty minutes of the initial phone call from the doctors.

When the doctor put Jordan on the phone, she cried, "Mommy, where is Daddy?" Again, I explained, "Daddy was hurt really badly, and he is at another place."

"Okay, but when are you going to get us out of here?"

I said, "I'll be there tomorrow. What do you want me to bring you?"

She answered, "A drink of water."

"Okay baby, we'll get you some. Be sweet, and remember, Mommy loves you, and I'll see you tomorrow, okay?"

It seems that my little Jamie, at the age of six, had made quite a name for herself in other ways, as well. Apparently, at the scene of the accident, while her father lay dead in the front seat of the SUV, and her sister lay next to her in the wreckage of the backseat, the state troopers found Jamie wounded, but alert enough to give them the information they needed. She was six years old! She told the authorities all of their names, my name, my cell phone number, and my mother's name and that she lived in Athens, TX. She even mentioned that I wasn't at home that I was at my sister's house, and then passed out. What a story. What a blessed little girl.

The police tried contacting me via my cell phone, but due to the bad weather and the location of the accident, they couldn't get a signal. But thank God for my daddy, and his daddy, and his daddy, and whoever branded us with such a one-of-a-kind surname. Because of the uniqueness of my maiden name, Kissentaner, the police called directory assistance in Athens, and did their best to re-pronounce the name the little girl had just spoken before passing out. - Because my hometown is so small, and *everybody* knows everybody, the police were notified, and they dispatched someone to Mama's house. But she was in Tyler, too.

So, there we were, doing everything we could, which, at our best, was nothing at all. I called my prayer partner from church to let her know what happened, and in turn, she contacted our pastor. Within minutes, my pastor, to whom I hadn't spoken in months because of my lingering anger, called to check on me. Not only did he check on me, he contacted his family in Oklahoma and other church members who had family in the area and asked them go to the hospital to check on my kids, until I could get there. He prayed with me and for me, and it was during his prayer that I thanked God that while I could have been tasked with making funeral arrangements for the kids, He allowed me to make flight arrangements, instead. I remembered that the girls and I would have one more thing in common — both our fathers died before either of us reached twelve years of age. I thought about my mother, who had lived long enough to bury two children, but thanked God that this wasn't my fate, this time.

I prayed for Martin's family, his parents and siblings. I could only imagine how devastating this must have been for them. I hadn't spoken to them in almost a year.

The next morning, I was finally able to make travel arrangements for Mama, Andy and me to fly to Oklahoma. The airports in Dallas were still closed, so Mama and I wouldn't be able to take the most direct route. I almost lost my cool with the reservations agent, as she quoted the most illogical flight schedules I had ever heard. But I was reminded this was our only option. We grabbed one day's worth of clothing and drove 250 miles south to Austin, picked up Andy and flew another 200 miles south to Houston and then to Tulsa. I could not understand for the life of me why the normal thirty-minute flight had to take us so far out of our way, of all days. Our plan was to pick up a car in Tulsa and drive the hour and a half to Stillwater. But God had other plans.

As we landed in Tulsa, the beauty of the snow blanketing the airport camouflaged the treacherous black ice underneath, which had caused the accident, ultimately killing Martin. The snow plows had cleared the runways and banks of snow towered more than fifteen feet high on either side of the freeway. Andy lamented, "That boy should have known to pull over. Look at this stuff." There was no anger in his voice, just wonder and amazement at how Martin and the kids made it this far. I was in shock and could say nothing.

As we walked through the airport toward the car rental desk, Andy's cell phone rang. Sissy was calling to tell us that Jordan's kidneys had begun to fail, and that both kids were being transferred to Tulsa by ambulance. (Look at GOD.) It was a bittersweet occasion because while I was concerned for

Jordie's health, I found relief in knowing we wouldn't have as far to drive under these conditions. As Jordan's health status decreased, and the decision was made to transport her, the emergency room physician in Stillwater demanded that the Tulsa hospital accept both kids because of all they had endured. With the safest drivers behind the wheel of the ambulance, the girls had been on the road to Tulsa for as long as we had been in flight to Tulsa, which was about three hours.

We were given directions to St. Francis Hospital and Andy carefully got us there. It was nearing 11:30 p.m. and I was exhausted, but determined to find my children. Talk about God's perfect timing? Driving up the ramp to the emergency room, an ambulance drove up the other side, meeting up with our car almost bumper to bumper. I was too consumed with worry to realize that this was the ambulance with the girls in it. I never noticed as they rolled the stretchers past us. I was more interested in finding the right people to get me to my children. The busybody was coming back…and there they were, Jordan and Jamie, right in front of me.

Again, God showed me how little my logic had to do with His planning, or His will. It was not His will for me to have a convenient flight, but in His timing, I would arrive at the same place where my children were, right at the same time. That's deep, huh?

I was not allowed to see them until we got into the hospital and presented identification and was debriefed about their injuries. It seemed as though the doctor rattled off medical terms for an hour, and frankly, I didn't care what he was saying. I just wanted my babies. Finally, they pulled back the curtain, and allowed us in.

The sight of my daughters on stretchers in the hospital emergency room remains indelibly etched into my memory. Is this what my mother felt like when Jane and Reuben died? No mother ever dreams of seeing her babies with any form of critical injury; but to see mine with dried blood matted in their sandy brown hair, and their beautiful innocent faces scarred, bruised and cut from broken glass, made me thank God that even in this state, they were still alive. They were as beautiful this way, as they were the first time I ever saw them. I had been given one more chance to do better for them. I had always been a pretty good mother to them, but that night I'll never forget my renewed commitment to these little ladies.

While in the airport, I had bought two rag dolls to take to them, hopefully to ease some of the pain they were about to go through, finding out about their dad. I leaned over the rail to kiss Jordan and gave her the doll, and as she licked her parched lips. Again she asked, "Where is Daddy?"

It looked as though she was locked in a straight jacket. But instead, it was a vest to secure her broken collarbone. She didn't move much as she talked to me. Her hazel eyes filled with tears and she tried to reach out for me, with apparent relief in her heart that we had finally arrived.

I tried not to ignore her, but stepped over toward Jamie's bed to hand her doll to her. Like her big sister, Jamie asked, "Where is Daddy, Mommy?" I reminded them both, "Daddy was hurt really badly and he is at another place." But as I looked into Jamie's eyes, I noticed something dreadfully wrong. They were crossed. For many reasons, we had to get that corrected, immediately. I asked the doctor, "What's wrong with her eyes?"

He answered, "What do you mean?"

I became agitated and snapped, "Look at her. Just look at her. Does she look normal to you?"

He apologized and answered, "That may indicate that she has a concussion. We'll get this checked out, right now."

She wore a neck brace and her arm was in a cast. She had more mobility than Jordan and was ready to get out of the bed, and into my arms. Reaching out for me she asked, "Mommy, when can we eat?"

I answered, "I don't know, but I'll find you something to eat in a while."

This was my confirmation of her well being, when she answered, "Good, because those folks at the other hospital would eat right there in front of us and wouldn't give us any, and we are starving, right Jordie?"

I chuckled to myself as I accepted their broken bones and fragile condition, but was reassured that their appetites were still strong. I then stepped back into my favorite role, Busybody Extraordinaire, as I set out to find them something to eat.

The attending physician chimed in, "We'll get these little ladies some crackers and water."

Jamie, overhearing the conversation, tried to rise up off the bed to find out if he was serious. She struggled with lifting the heavy neck brace as she winced from the pain and plopped back down softly onto the pillow.

"Crackers and water?" she piped up. "Mommy, did he just say crackers and water? I'm hungry. I want some meat."

That's the real Jamie. She was without a doubt on her way to being all right. This was the first time I had laughed in almost two days. Mama and Andy laughed with me, as we shook our heads in amazement at our funny little hero. Andy whispered to her that he would go out and find all of us something to eat, and bring it back, but they had to promise to stay up for him. They promised and he left.

Thirty minutes later, the nurse showed up with the crackers and water, and although the girls were not impressed, they devoured them. They had missed a traditional Christmas dinner and hadn't eaten in thirty-six hours. Instead, they substituted the turkey, dressing and trimmings for two crackers and a couple of sips of water. On her way out the door, the nurse peered over her chained bifocals to caution me, "I know your *husband* went to get them some food, but they can't have it."

That was the one time that I wanted to act ignut. How was she going to tell me that I couldn't give *my* children something to eat, when they were hungry? Obviously, she didn't know the story, or maybe she did. Never acknowledging her comment, I just thought to myself, *Woman, please!* Apparently, the reciprocating look I gave her told her what was on my heart. She walked away mumbling, "Just don't give them too much. It may make them sick."

Sure enough, a few minutes later, the sound of rustling bags in the hallway was Uncle Andy. He walked into the room with his arms full of food from Denny's. It was the only place still open, and from the look the bags he had with him, he apparently bought one of everything they had. As he sat the bags down on the table, he asked, "Why did that nurse roll her eyes at me, as I walked by her?" Again, I chuckled to myself.

After having our own holiday feast complete with pancakes, sausage, eggs, hash browns, a grilled ham and cheese sandwich, and a cheeseburger, we all felt better. I encouraged Andy and Mama to go and check into the hotel. I would spend the night with the girls in their room. I couldn't leave them there alone. It had been a long day, and I wanted Andy and Mama to get some rest. They agreed and left us at about 1 o'clock in the morning.

The girls' beds were set up on opposing walls so when one needed me, I'd have to walk across the room to her bedside. When I'd walk away to check on her needs, the other would cry out, "Mommy, don't leave me, please."

Needless to say, I couldn't equally divide my time between the two of them. This was about to get difficult. I couldn't sleep with one and not the other. When one asked for a drink, the other needed one as well. For the first thirty minutes, I walked back and forth between them, trying to comfort them in every way I could. That's when it dawned on me that Martin was really dead. This was when I realized parenting is a job for two people. Though the distance between my children was only a mere fifteen feet, my trying to attend to both of them was almost impossible.

In previous times, when I had teetered on the edge of screaming, somehow, like a knight in shining armor, he would show up to take over for me. Like when Jamie was diagnosed with pneumonia, and was transported from one hospital to another, he left his field exercises and drove more than two hours to Dallas to make sure we were okay. Another time, when Jordan was a toddler, she detached two of her fingertips in a freak accident. Upon getting the message from the military police, Martin ran two of the four miles back to the post to meet us at the hospital. Not this time. I was by myself; just me and these two little girls, without their daddy.

As much as I tried to soothe the girls and reassure them, I couldn't continue the to-and-fro dance I had begun. With tears in my voice, I spoke up, "Girls, I'm trying to take care of both of you, right now and it's tough because your beds are so far apart. I know you are scared, because I am too, but now, everything is going to be okay. So, I'm going to pull this chair away from the wall, and set it in the middle of the room so both of you can see me and I'll be close to both of you, okay?"

I continued, "I'm going to turn down the lights and turn the television to *Nick at Nite,* and we can all go to sleep, okay?"

Jordan answered, "Okay, Mommy, but can I please have another drink before we go night-night?"

"Me, too, Mommy," Jamie added.

The drink of water the girls and I shared in the ICU was physically refreshing and symbolically nourishing as well. Nearing our fortieth hour of distress, we were finally together again. They were so extremely dehydrated because they had been restricted from eating or drinking anything for forty hours. Nothing to drink or eat, no parents, no one, for forty hours.

{Please press PAUSE} In the Bible, the number forty always represents a trial before a triumph (forty-day flood, forty years in the desert, forty days of temptation). Stay tuned for the triumph. Here it comes. {Press PLAY, please}

But when they were finally able to drink water, I was permitted to give it to them. Not some stranger, but their mother was able to give them *free water*. We all sipped from the same cup, and then it meant very little, but in hindsight it represented how our family unit, would do *everything* together – grieving, healing, laughing, talking, eating, sleeping, and the list goes on. But the sip of water was the beginning of our new life, committed to loving each other, for real.

The chair in the pediatric ICU room that I placed in the middle of the floor between both girls' beds for me to sleep became my thinking chair and my praying chair. It is in that chair that I had to pray and ask God for direction and strength on how to break the devastating news of their father's death to them. *What would I say? How would I do it?* I don't know where that chair is now, but it was the most uncomfortable chair I have ever sat, thought, prayed and slept in. Not literally speaking, but figuratively. I hope to never have to sit there again.

***

When the sun peeked through the curtains of our room, I was already awake. I spent most of the night awake, wondering just what to do. The girls slept, though I don't know how comfortably; they rested all night.

As they awakened, I washed their faces, and helped them to brush their teeth, supporting their backs as they strained to sit up. I couldn't comb their hair because of the many cuts in their heads. Nonetheless, I did my best to make them look like the little angels they were.

The hospital sent a social worker to me to discuss our family's situation. When I asked her for direction on how to break the news to the kids, the polite and petite blonde woman held my hand and kindly said, "Ma'am, I'm sorry, but I can't help you with this one. You know your children better than anyone else. There's no right or wrong way to do it, and either method will not change what we all know. I can't tell you how. You have to do what you feel is best. But if you'd like me to be here with you, I will."

Well, thanks a lot, I thought, while trying not to send a discouraging message to her. I didn't know what to do, or how to do it, or what to say.

Mama and Andy, my relief team, came in as the social worker and I finished our conversation. As she walked toward the door, she looked back at me with a smile, and said,

"I think you've got all the help you need, not just in your family, but in God, as well. Here's my business card, if you need me."

Uncle Andy continued in his usual antics to make the girls laugh, while their grandmother helped them with their breakfast. Thank God for a family. I was about ready to cry when they came in, just when I needed them most.

With no words planned in mind, I went to Jamie's bed first and sat down with her. I held her hand and softly spoke words to her, much like Mama had done to me twenty-one years earlier. "Jamie, you know about the accident you were in with Daddy, right."

"Yes, ma'am."

"Okay, I've got to tell you something, and I need for you to be a big girl, and try to understand, okay?

"Yes, ma'am."

"Daddy didn't make it out of the accident. He died."

Tears welled up in her eyes, but she said nothing. She acted just like Emmaline and Patrice. She didn't say a word. Grieving tears gushed from her eyes while she looked at me, but still she said nothing.

"Jamie, I need for you to be strong for me because Jordie's injuries are worse than yours, so I had to tell you first. Okay? Can you help me to help Jordie, again?

"Umm humm," she said, as she nodded her head while trying to dry her eyes.

"He died for real?"

"Yes, Baby," as I leaned over to kiss her and to wipe away her tears.

"Where is he, now?"

"He's still in Stillwater where you had the accident."

"Is he at the hospital?"

"No, he's at a funeral home."

"What happened?"

"We don't know everything yet, but when I know more, I'll tell you what I can. Okay?"

"Yes ma'am."

"Are you okay, Sweetie?"

"Yes."

"It's okay for you to cry, but remember, Daddy is in heaven now."

"Okay." She sobbed quietly and held my hand, as she wiped away her own tears.

One down and one to go. It wasn't as bad as I thought it would be. Jamie again proved her maturity level exceeded her years. She was okay. If it worked once, hopefully it would work again with Jordan. With more courage, I walked toward Jordan's bed to talk to her.

"Jordie, I need to talk to you for a minute."

"Yes ma'am," her voice still hoarse.

"I know you know about the accident, huh? I've got something to tell you that's pretty hard to say, but I've got to do it."

"Yes ma'am?"

"Daddy died in the car accident."

Unlike her sister, she frowned at me as though she wanted to curse me. Still in pain from her broken clavicle, she rolled her eyes at me, and strained to turn and face the wall.

With a shaky voice, she demanded to know, "When is his funeral? What color is his casket?"

I answered, "Sweetheart, none of that has been decided yet. I don't know."

"I want him to have a silver casket."

"Okay, I'll call Big Mama to see if she has picked one out, and if not, maybe she can get a silver one."

The call to Martin's parents was the last time Jordan would talk to me for the next hour. His mother spoke to Jordan and assured her that she would honor her wish, and select a silver coffin for him.

Jordan shut the world out. She refused to drink anything or talk to anyone else. Not me, the nurses, her sister or Mama. The television stayed on Nickelodeon, and her eyes remained fixed on the screen, as though no one else was there. It was only when Uncle Andy asked them if they wanted an ice-cream cone, did she respond. He didn't care that the girls had just finished breakfast no more than an hour before. "If they want ice-cream, we're getting ice cream. So what kind do y'all want?"

"I'ont know; whatever kind they have is okay," Jamie replied.

Jordan was more specific with her request. "I want a bomb pop."

So, he set out to find a bomb pop and anything else cool and satisfying for his nieces. Like the night before, he didn't return to the room until he accomplished his mission.

Just like I knew he would, my brother helped me when I couldn't think of the right thing to do. And like when I was a child, ice-cream always made me feel better, and apparently had not lost its potency on children. Andy bought himself an ice-cream cone as well, and they had a contest to see who could finish theirs first. He won.

That's just how Andy is. The night of Reuben's death, when we went to dinner at Luby's in Oak Cliff, the children ordered Jell-O for dessert. Andy taught all of the kids how to put Jell-O into their mouths and squish it through their teeth. Yeah it was nasty-looking and gross, but he had fun showing the kids how to do it. Not once, but they did it over and over until they ran out of Jell-O. Today, he's still an eight-year-old trapped in a forty-two-year-old body. Once again, I was reminded of just how fortunate I am to have had two great brothers in my life.

As the girls continued to show progress, their conditions were upgraded and they were moved from the intensive care unit to a regular room. Jamie was ready to get out of bed and find something else to do. She had had it with being cooped up. She hated the neck brace and told the doctor, "You can go ahead and take this off of me now. I'm fine."

When he told her to keep it on for another day, she asked, "What time tomorrow will you be here to take it off?"

He had met his match. Jamie needed an answer, so that she would know. He laughed and said, "I'll stop by your room first."

Sure enough, he did. Jordan's recovery was a little slower and consequently, when Jamie was finally able to get up and move around, Jordie remained bed ridden. Her granny stayed at her bedside. When the nurses removed Jamie's catheter, she and I took a walk around the hospital. We found the hospital cafeteria, and she decided that this is where we would have dinner that evening, rather than in their room. "Let's go and get dressed and come back down here to eat." (I guess she thought it was a restaurant.)

I compromised, "Why don't we order something now, and take it back to the room to share with Jordan and Granny?"

After a moment of consideration, she replied, "Well, I guess that's a good idea."

She ordered dinner for all of us. "We'll have the barbecued chicken, macaroni and cheese, a cheeseburger, French fries, chef salad, fish sticks and chicken nuggets and four sprites." My baby was still hungry, and so was I. We almost needed a cart to take it all back to the room.

That night, I was finally able to sleep. I had been allowed to check into the Ronald McDonald house, where I never turned on the light or the television in the room. As I plopped down onto the bed, fully dressed, I drifted off to sleep. I slept so soundly that when morning came, I thought I had slept through the next day, with my sneakers and coat still on. I hadn't realized how exhausted I was.

Over the course of the next two days, the girls' conditions improved and we were given the okay for traveling. I was ready for the trip when I realized the children had no shoes or coats to wear because they were destroyed in the accident. This meant I had to go out into the dangerous weather to shop. This was not a diva's shopping spree, but an essential one, instead. Thankfully, K-Mart was right around the corner.

After getting to the airport, returning the car, buying the tickets and helping the girls onto the aircraft, I was thankful that the worst was behind us. It didn't matter that we all couldn't sit together. Mama took Jordan, and I took Jamie, and we made it home. I was not concerned when I discovered that our baggage didn't make the flight. Who cared? I had my children and we were finally safe at home.

My pastor and his loving wife met us at the airport in the church van to bring us home. They brought balloons and bears for the girls, and did what caring and loving Christians do. They offered us themselves, for whatever we needed. Likewise, our church congregation did the same. This time, when I was in need, people came to my rescue; just like it had happened for my parents when Jane died.

Do you even remember Christmas 2000? Do you know what you got for Christmas that year? While you were having dessert, I was feeling deserted. While your children were riding bikes, mine rode in an ambulance. I don't recall having a gift under the Christmas tree that year. But the gifts I received could never be wrapped — a real relationship with God, a second chance with my children, renewed family ties, peace, and wisdom. Thank you, God for giving me what I needed, and not what I wanted. Just another Christmas? Not hardly.

Chapter

9 "Yield Not to Temptation"

Fast-forward to January 6, 2001, as we lined up to walk into our church for the funeral of my ex-husband (of two weeks). The bad weather delayed the service for nearly two weeks. Outside, the weather was cold. My children were still in casts and slings, unable to put their coats on, but they instead wore them like capes to shield them from the 40 degree climate. The eleven o'clock sunshine provided brilliant light, but little warmth from the whipping winter winds.

I was unable to hug or hold the girls as we walked in because Jamie's left arm was in a cast, and Jordan's left clavicle was broken, and she still wore a sling. So, I placed my arms around their shoulders just to convey, "Mommy is here with you." I could only imagine what was going through their saddened and frightened minds. There lay the man of their dreams — the handsome soldier, the one who sneaked candy to them against Mommy's wishes, their private basketball and soccer coach — their everything lay in a casket, which we slowly walked toward at the altar. The silver casket, Jordan picked out.

soccer coach — their everything lay in a casket, which we slowly walked toward at the altar. The silver casket, Jordan picked out.

The sanctuary was over capacity. Those who could find a spot inside hurried in to escape the cold. People sat in the fellowship hall, the foyer and even more stood huddled together outside to brave the cutting January winds. Jamie's soccer team was there in uniform. The army was there, dressed for the ceremony. Our choir loft overflowed with members, respectfully dressed in black. Friends, who I thought had forgotten about me, were there. The post office was there. Our church family was there. Martin's huge family was there, and a great portion of my tribe was there, too. I was comforted as Sissy and Andy sat with me and the girls, with the rest of Martin's family. As I helped the girls remove their coats, and we took our seats, guess who walked in? Her. The Tender Eyed She Devil. And guess where she sat? Four rows behind his children and me.

{Please press PAUSE…and keep it there for a moment.}

Can you imagine what was running through my mind? A few scriptures popped into my thinking, *Get thee behind me Satan!* I desperately tried to remember Jamie's rendition of a Sunday School memory verse, which she quoted so eloquently, "Resist the devil because he has fleas." I couldn't think of it. Evil thoughts consumed me. I contemplated kicking her as she symbolically and literally walked between the front row pew where I sat, and Martin's coffin. Once again, there she was coming between us. I wanted to kick her dead in the back seam of her skirt — right in her rear, as she walked by — just a gentle nudge to help her to her seat. Not. I wanted to hurt her, both physically and emotionally.

Another soul-saving opportunity flashed before my eyes, as I wanted to beat the hell out of her. (I'm just telling you the truth. Remember, confession is good for the soul.) I thought about just jumping up and choking the snot out of her, knowing that my girlfriends who were there with me would have joined the melee. They wanted to whip her just as much as I did. I wanted to tear down flowers and pull out her hair by the handfuls. I saw myself taking a swing at her; landing one right in her beady little eyes. My diva status didn't matter. (Diva's rule number two: *Look good in everything you do.*) I didn't care about my new suit, sunglasses or my new shoes. Forget the graceful diva, I had come to be, I wanted to revert to "ghetto ninja." It didn't matter that I didn't know how to fight, I was willing to learn, right there in the comfort of my church. I wanted to humiliate her for all the dirty things she had done to me for the past seven years. For that very moment, my senses of humor, compassion and forgiveness escaped me.

I thought about asking the funeral director to kindly pause the service and escort the little devil out of my church, so that our family could grieve and get through this funeral. I also considered going up to the podium to look that devil straight in her crooked little eyes, and to tell her exactly what I thought of her…in front of all of God's children. There are three reasons why I didn't:

1. My children.

2. I didn't want to bring any shame to Martin's memory, in front of so many people.

3. My mama.

All I could hear was my mother's voice, from two nights earlier, "Patrice, you put this in God's hands and he'll take care of it better than you can. He'll make your enemies your footstool. You just give this mess to God." So, again, I did nothing. She (the devil) got another one in on me...for a moment. She was winning.

Meanwhile, a few rows behind me, and unbeknownst to me, I learned that she was experiencing her own grief, as she tried to find a seat. None of my family or friends would make room for her. Teeheehee (God forgive me, please.) {Press PLAY}

When water was free, the other woman sat at the back of the church with a dark veil on, black gloves and carried a single rose. They didn't have the guts to make themselves seen in public...and certainly weren't silly enough to show up at church and sit with the bereaved family. Ya know, like on the "Lifetime" movies? Maybe she doesn't have cable because Ms. Thang found a prominent seat down front, just a few feet away from me. She managed to slither into a place, and sat there uncomfortably for the entire three hours. What was going through her stupid little head?

Very few people knew that we were actually divorced, and most of those who spoke of him, talked about his undying love for our children and me. One soldier, who approached the podium, spoke of Martin as his boss, but more importantly as his friend. He shared that they talked about everything, good and bad. They knew each others lives, inside and out. With tears in his eyes, but a gigantic smile in his voice, he looked over at me and proclaimed, "Patrice, I want you to know that there's not another woman *anywhere* that he loved more than he loved you."

Take that devil! I thought to myself. I so desperately wanted to stand up, turn around, and in juvenile folly, poke my tongue out at her, perhaps roll my eyes at her, work my neck, turn up my nose at her, and give her the hand just to let her know that the score was changing and that I had been right all along. But I didn't.

I smiled as he finished his remarks, and nodded to him as a kind and heartfelt "thank you" for his words. Meanwhile, Old Tender Eyes was getting a bit emotional, with the constant references to Martin's love for me. My mother was right. I started to feel better, as she began to squirm under the pressure, while God began making her my footstool. My mama is so smart.

Vengeance was not mine, that day, although I wanted a big slice of it, right out of her tail. As the service progressed, she finally broke down and cried as my girlfriend Tracy's sixteen-year-old daughter leaned over and whispered to her, "Don't you feel pretty stupid, now?"

After everything was over, and I had a moment of repentance, I tried to get in touch with her because I wanted to apologize for my part in gloating while she looked so foolish. Although it brought me great joy, I knew it wasn't right. Like a vulture, she had swooped into town, looking for someone to prey on. Like a serpent, she spread her poisonous venom on anyone who would listen. That's how the devil works; he takes a little bit and plays on our emotions when we are at our weakest. Like me, Martin's family was grieving, and she knew that she could win them over with a lie, and hope for some sympathy. It almost worked.

She had tricked his family into believing that they were engaged to be married. Well, maybe she was marrying him, but I'm not certain he was going to marry her. Here's why I feel this way. Remember his Christmas gift to me? Now, you are the judge, if he were going to marry her, why didn't *she* get the policy? I don't know either.

Chapter

10 "Why I Didn't Cry"

Emotions raging as waves on a stormy ocean. Constant. Fierce. Crashing. Breaking. High. Low. Predictable. Dangerous. A calm lull in the tempest. Nothing.

The storm re-energizes. Apathy. Anger. Fear. Frustration. Dismay. Disdain. Gratitude. Attitude. Love and Hate. The storm continues. Nothing.

A stronger more violent storm churns, not on the seas, not on land, but in the dank, dreary cave between the teeth. The pink tornado rages, tearing down homes, isolating families, destroying trust, and breeding mischief. Gossip. Lies. Plans. Schemes. Plots. Greed. Lack. Give. Take. Share. Need. Expectations. The storm pauses. Nothing.

My mama doesn't cry much; consequently, neither do I. Ignorantly, I never knew the rest of the free world measured love in the amount of tears shed, until I learned of the criticisms hurled at me when I didn't cry at his funeral. From behind the printed obituaries and fans, my watchers whispered, "Look at her, she don't even care."

"She ain't cried, yet."

"Umm hmmm, she acts like she's glad."

"When she gon' cry?"

No, I didn't cry, and while I didn't feel I had to explain my actions to anyone, I never even thought about crying. Although I understand my critics' assessment of my performance at the funeral, they needed to know that inside, I was dealing with issues more close to my heart than they, the funeral goers, the Kleenex-counting grief measurers could ever fathom.

My life had drastically changed.

He was dead.

Thank God we had just renewed our friendship with each other for the sake of our children.

He was dead.

He had just offered to tell "Tender Eyes" to take a hike, in an effort to restore his family. (And I didn't necessarily believe it, until the insurance policies totaling over $300,000 were paid to me.)

He was dead.

I hadn't spoken to his parents in nearly a year.

He was dead, but not for eternity. He had acknowledged Christ early in life, so I knew he was resting in the arms of his Savior. So, overlooking the destruction of the mangled SUV, and the tragedy of my children's lives without their dad, we were still blessed. The most important fact about all that happened was overlooked. He was in heaven and our children were alive. My children were alive. I had another chance to build a relationship with his parents, despite all that had happened. No tears. No explanations. No regrets about my relationship with him; only thanksgiving for things being as well as they were.

So, as the soloist sang "My Soul Has Been Anchored in The Lord," I stood with my arms extended heavenward. I rejoiced, but with closed, dry eyes. I remained unaware that I was being graded by a few bored people.

Those who had taken no time to learn about the situation, sat unaware of my family's familiarity with the death angel. They didn't know how we grieved. They didn't know our secret for dealing with death. The best thing I could do was accept God's will at Martin's death, without the "why" questions. For I've found out, there are rarely acceptable answers to such unending questions. As I sat there in front of yet another flag-draped coffin holding someone else dear to my heart, I had to apply everything I knew about death being a powerless, but obedient servant of God. I had to remind myself of the good times, like when we slow danced in each other's arms, and when we became parents. I had to try and forget about the woman seated a few rows behind me. Yes, I had to "look to the hills..."

Was that fair to me? No.

Did it hurt me? Yes.

Could I do anything about it? No.

But I tried, and nearly lost everything I had while attempting to prove to the naysayers that my heart harbored no bitterness toward anyone. Nevertheless, from my anger toward them, and rather than confronting anyone, I penned this poem to appease their hungry appetites and my desire to be heard:

Why I Didn't Cry

Dedicated to my Kappa man in the sky. January 2001

Don't ask me why, why didn't I cry -
My husband of nine years was dead.
Our kids survived the accident, and lived, instead.
Don't ask me why, why I didn't cry...
Somebody had to be strong.

Christmas Day- peace on earth, good will toward men,
But God looked down, and took my best friend.
I was at my sister's house some 400 miles away,
While in pediatric ICU, is where our kids lay.
Don't ask me why, why I didn't cry...
Somebody had to be strong.

A wonderful father, and a handsome Kappa man,
My soul mate for life, but God had other plans.
Don't ask me why, why I didn't cry...
For this was God's will.

Did I mention we were divorced for a whole two weeks?
Yeah, we had allowed the enemy to throw us a curve,
And instead of working it out, I just had him served!
And in retrospect, I now realize...it wasn't that serious!
Don't ask me why, why I didn't cry...
And even through all of that, he was still my best friend.

His last hours on earth, he spent with me and our girls,
Nothing could have been more perfect for his last day
in this world.
Mommy and Daddy and the kids and toys,
Hugs and kisses, everyone filled with Christmas joy.
As they left for Kansas, my children and my best friend,
We agreed that when he returned, we'd be a family again.
Don't ask me why, why I didn't cry...
This was our destiny.

I'm now a single black mother, raising two beautiful girls,
Physically alone, in a cold and hateful world.
But we had planned our kids' lives,
Where they'd go to college, and what they'd drive
So don't ask me why, why I didn't cry...
We had done our homework.

But you see, I did cry, but it was one year later,
As I realized the truth could never be greater.
The silence in our house was too great to bear…
When I wanted to hear from him, no one was there
When the phone stopped ringing and the funeral food was gone,
I wept to myself, for I knew this meant I'd be alone.

Tears filled with love rolled down my cheeks and face,
Reminding me that there's not another man anywhere,
who could ever take his place.
My boo, my baby and my lover for life,
The most treasured days I've lived, were when I was his wife.

But life goes on; I recognize what it means to be loved,
And settle for less than any of God's best, is something I'd never dream of.
So, I thank God for my Kappa man, who is dwelling in the sky,
Who helps me to remember, that I don't have to cry.

Because everything we needed to do, we completed before he went home,
Now it's up to me, to ensure that his dream continues on.
My last time to speak with him on this side of glory,
But it was just another chapter in our beautiful story.
So, don't ask me why, why I didn't cry.
I was blessed just to know him.

Yes, I grieved silently without the critical eyes of the watchers. At home by myself, when the crowds were gone, I wept. At work, locked behind my office door, I cried. In line at the grocery store, when nothing was wrong, I stood there and cried. While watching the girls as they recovered from their injuries, I cried. Seeing them overcome by life without their father, I cried. Silently, I wondered if they would have to endure the humiliation of a cruel comment made about me, such as "Something's wrong with her, because she grew up without her father." I prayed that I would be able to raise the children alone and protect them from evil thoughts such as this lurking around them. But the critics never saw that. All they saw was me praising God for his goodness toward my children, which according to their standards was inappropriate. And further credit to their lack of knowledge is the fact that I didn't cry at my daddy's funeral, and he was *my first love*.

***

Over the next twelve months, I upgraded our home, put away money for our children's college, took the girls on a couple of Mommy and Daughter trips and bought a new car. After that, I gave away every dime he had left to me. I'll give you a second to think about it, and the amount of money we are talking about.

"Who in their right mind would do that?" That's a good question. I wasn't in my right mind, but I still gave it all away.

To whom? Anyone who asked.

To pay for what? House payments, rent payments, late car payments, down payments on cars (including one dump truck, which I've never seen), investments in three businesses, with no return on any of them, cash gifts to those in need, lavish birthday gifts, airline tickets, you name it. It felt good to help out those whom I love. It wasn't just my family or friends; it was anybody who came to me, in need — his family, in-laws, out-laws. It didn't matter to me. Besides, if he were alive, he would have given it away, too.

Why? To let everyone know that I was still a good person. Also because I had received an unexpected "endowment," I felt it was the right thing for me to do. I did not keep any of it for myself, and again be talked about for my insensitivity. Somehow, I had overlooked the often quoted proverb, "A fool and his money are soon parted." How do you spell fool? G-E-O-R-G-I-A P-A-T-R-I-C-E K-I-S-S-E-N-T-A-N-E-R.

What I didn't give away, was lost post- 9/11, as September 11, 2001 nearly bankrupted me. Practically standing on the front steps of foreclosure of my home, I re-traced my steps back to many of those who I had helped. I was shunned and given excuses, three hot checks, and grief for pleading to them for their help. Most of the people to whom my blessings flowed moved on quietly with their lives, and I rarely, if ever, saw them anymore. From the thousands of dollars I handed out, I received $672.00 in return. Disappointed and embarrassed, but humbled by it all, I remained thankful to those who sent what they did. We desperately needed it.

This time when I cried, I wasn't angry, but hurt again. My children were depending on me, and I let them down. I was counting on others worse off than me. I maintained my faith in God and tithed what I had left, but wondered how long it would be this way. I hurt for everybody involved, not just for myself and my poor judgment. This was an unfamiliar and extremely difficult growing pain; even so, I earned another blessing and learned a valuable lesson from this incident. Don't lend money that you cannot afford to give. I then wondered, *Had my wisdom teeth been pulled too early?*

Everything and everyone whom I had come to depend on was gone. My life's pruning had happened. Just as the flowers in Mama's yard, I had to be trimmed, and cut. Martin, and the childhood friends and new acquaintances who I thought I had bought and paid for with the money he left for me, all were but a memory. My pride was gone. My trust for people in general declined, and I had never felt lower in my life. If my mother had had any clue of what I was doing with the money, she probably would have shot me point blank, just to put me out of my upcoming misery. But life is far more than money and friends. Life is worthless if you have no peace. When I finally came to my senses and talked to her about my situation, she was ready to listen. "Right there, on her front porch, in the quietness and stillness of an east Texas breeze, we chatted. The same home where all three of her children, and two grandchildren had grown up and left, I was back there, again. Safe from myself, my bad decisions and heartaches, I was back in the "mayor's office," with her undivided attention."

In addition to offering her support, she reminded me, "First things first. Honey, you don't owe anybody any explanation for anything you do. You're a grown woman. You didn't owe anybody any of that money, including me. He left that to you and those kids, and if he felt that way, who cares what anybody else thinks? Now that you're broke, things are going to look a little different to you, but watch what I tell you, you're still gon' come out on top. Those of us, who love you, don't need an explanation for what you do. And those who mean you no good ain't gon' believe you anyway. So, don't worry about this, we'll get through it. And you've got to always remember just how you are hurting right now, so you won't make this mistake again."

She dried my tears and hugged me in a way that reminded me of Diva's rule number three: *Ain't nobody but God, Mama and me.*

But wait, there's more.

The likelihood of me getting remarried remained as unlikely as a senior Republican Senator reporting to special session wearing gold teeth and Fubu gear and sneakers. So, when a friend invited me to a wedding in November 2001, I never dreamed Love would find me there. At first sight, I had no idea this is what Love really looked like. Love didn't fit my spec sheets. While I preferred a fairer toned, taller and thinner companion, Love was a 212-pound chunk of Omega-type chocolate.

Love had his eyes on me, and I was not the least bit interested. According to him, I had put up a smoke screen which intimidated the weaker brothers at the wedding, but he wasn't fazed by it. He said he knew like King Solomon, I was his "good thing." (Proverbs 18:22) I would be his, and it would only be a matter of time. Yeah, yeah, yeah. After three months of persistence, he invited me to lunch, and I was pleasantly amused to find Like, which later turned to Love.

My daddy would have had a great time making "colored fun" about my Love's immaculately beautiful brown skin. I am certain; however, that once Daddy knew just how much Love makes me smile, he'd love Love almost as much as I do. Likewise, I introduced Mama to Love, and she immediately liked him, and was captivated by his big heart and grand smile — a smile big as our Lone Star State. He's from Corsicana, which is only thirty-six miles from Athens; so he's from the country, too, just like me. We knew lots of the same people, and are surprised that our lives' paths hadn't crossed earlier. In his job, he traveled around the country, and lived in Taiwan and Venezuela for a few months. How then, had we both traveled so much, only to find each other at this time in our lives? It was our time.

Introducing him to the girls was a big deal for me because he had to meet their approval first. I needed only to set up the meeting. Real love did the rest. Immediately, there was a bond established between Love and the girls, and my heart was overjoyed, especially because I had nothing to do its success.

Love loved me when I had very little to offer him. He cared for me when I couldn't emotionally care for myself. He made me laugh. Love reminded me of how difficult and mean life can be, only if we allow it to be. He accepted me as the wounded but loving person I was. No pretenses, no false hopes, no strings attached, he simply gave me the only thing he had: Himself.

That's when Like really turned into Love. After coming through our storm, finding Love was the last thing on my mind, but the best thing to ever happen to me. As you and I have learned, I'm not in control of too much these days.

As a result, Love is my best friend and I am so thankful for another chance at true love. And this time, I know who I am, what to expect, how to react, and how not to give up. Ours is a relationship much like that of Cadillac Red and the "whippersnapper." We love each other, with a mature love, and everything we do is based solely upon that love. We trust each other because we share a great friendship. When my husband doesn't understand, I can talk to him, as my friend, and it seems to work out just fine.

We were married April 20, 2003. We were both unemployed by June 13, 2003. We didn't care. We had each other, our children, our severance packages and a whole bunch of love. Love has a teenaged son and a god daughter and god son who are both just as kind and loving as their dad. So we have a great "Brady Bunch" family.

Through a series of divine appointments, while unemployed, Love met a friendly stranger at jury duty, who invited him into his world. The kind stranger then introduced him to an abundantly blessed business man; let's just call him "Mack," who offered him a job, doing what he loves.

In the beginning of this book, I confessed my apparent misunderstanding in who would "give unto my bosom," when I had given so much to others. Now, I know that many blessings come from people who we won't always know, like "Mack." Just like my Love, I believe "Mack" to be one of the "good men whose steps are ordered by God." Now, Love works in a dream job, doing what he has longed to do since leaving his profession.

And me? I'm just happy. I'm mothering, I'm wifing, I'm working, I'm ushering, I'm writing, I'm cooking, and we are traveling. I'm doing the things that bring me joy and contentment.

As a result of my painful but timely pruning, I have blossomed again, and there are more roses in my life now, than I've ever been aware of. They've been around all along, but now, I notice them, and they smell just a little sweeter to me. I'm speaking of my family, who I've always loved, but never told them just how much.

So, when people see me walking around with this big honeymoon grin eternally plastered to my face, I don't worry what they think. I am happy again. I'm at peace with me, and God, and I don't worry about too much anymore. I haven't tried to solve anyone's issues in over a year. Love changed all of that for me.

"And we lived happily ever after..."

Chapter 11 "Choices and Changes"

My life can best be summarized as what Paul wrote to the church at Rome, "All things work together for the good of them who love the Lord, and are called according to his purpose." What things work together for your good, you ask? Victories, losses, life, death, successes, failures, other women, mean people, wonderful people, good advice, bad advice, thieves, angels, truth and deception....all these things have worked together— much like the Aqua Net, Dippity-Do, and Royal Crown — to tame me and hold me in place, until I can get to my destination.

This book could have been entitled, "Waaahh, waaahh, waaahh, Why Has Life Been So Mean to Me?" or "Memories from A Bitter Woman's Tongue" but I chose, "When Water Was Free," because I'm not angry or bitter. I'm happy to be alive, married and content. I continue to choose to remember the happiest of times. The choices I make are to be happy and content where I am. I have witnessed enough sorrows, death and tragedy in my life that if I wanted to, I could cry myself into insanity. I could threaten to take my own life. I could focus on all the times I didn't make the mark. All are devious tricks of the enemy.

Rather than become angered each time I see someone drunk, whose liver is functioning without fail, I remember that cancer respects no one. Cancer didn't care that my father did not drink alcohol in excess, but cirrhosis of the liver took away the life of my favorite guy. Rather than try to figure out how Jane died, I thank God for sending Andy and Sissy to be my brother and sister. Instead of being mad at God for taking my only biological brother away from me, I'm thankful that he put off heaven a few hours for his baby sister. I don't spend my time focusing on the infidelity of my former spouse, but instead the wonderful "porkin bean" memories we shared. Without meditating on the memories of outgrown friendships, I now look at how I've been blessed with a new husband who is my best friend. Those are all conscious choices I make. But lest you become distracted and surmise that this book is still only about me, you've missed it. Go back and start over again.

Earlier in the book, I quoted Deuteronomy 29:29, mentioned, "the secret things belong unto the Lord..." and promised to share proof of that statement with you. For about a year after Martin's death, like many, I wondered about the truth of the accident. What really happened? Did someone else see something? Who called 9-1-1? The only person who I thought would know anything about it would be my baby Jamie, and I wouldn't dare take her back through the pain of recalling any part of it. So, I left it alone, putting it back into God's hands, realizing in His appointed time, I would know what He felt I needed to know, when I could handle it.

In the summer of 2002, I accepted a temporary assignment at a travel agency, working for three weeks. The office was okay, although I was over qualified for the position. The staff was pleasant, and the young lady assigned to help me was eager to do so. We sat across from each other, and formed a corporate friendship, as she helped me to become familiar with policies. One day she joined me for lunch. While I drove, we made small talk about our likes, but concentrated on our dislikes about north Dallas traffic. While stopped at red light, she brought up a conversation about driving in bad weather. It went like this:

"Patrice, it was about noon one Christmas while driving home from Oklahoma, when we saw what had to have been the worst accident I've ever seen in my life. There was a silver-looking SUV that had been hit by another truck, right in the driver's side door, and the other vehicle that looked like it had been in the accident was further up the road. We were on Interstate 35, out in the middle of nowhere, but not too far from Oklahoma City. The weather was so bad; we couldn't stop in time to see if the people were okay. I couldn't get over what I saw because it was Christmas Day. I knew somebody was hurt really badly."

When I explained our family's story to her, she burst into tears apologizing, "I didn't pull over! Patrice, I'm sorry. We should have stopped."

I reassured her, "It's understandable. It's okay. Everything happens for a reason, and apparently, you weren't supposed to have pulled over."

She never relented, "I'm so sorry, Patrice."

I never stopped telling her, "I understand."

The whole thing was rather bizarre for me, but until that point, I had never realized exactly why I had been sent to the agency to work.. Her statements confirmed for me my purpose in her office was not for my career advancement, but rather an answer to a prayer I had prayed months before. More than two years had passed since the accident but I learned that my family wasn't there on the highway for hours, alone and suffering.

We ordered our lunch, but never ate it. Returning to our desks, she didn't talk much that afternoon, and consequently, my assignment ended early. When I left, I sent a message to her thanking her for all of her help while I was there, and extending a lifelong thank you for helping to put some of my questions to rest.

Isn't that an awesome story? We never know who we may meet in our daily walk through life. We may come across someone who holds an answer to the unanswered questions in life. I remain thankful that of all the out-of-work travel agents in the Dallas area, I was selected for the assignment, and was fortunate enough to sit across from the one who could help me. The secret things do belong unto the Lord.

Now unto him that is able to keep you from falling and to present you faultless before the presence of his glory with exceeding joy, To the only wise God our Savior, be glory and majesty, dominion and power, both now and forever. Amen (Jude 1:24-25).

Chapter

12 "People, Places, Things and Ideas"

Dear Jordan and Jamie,

You have just read a little about a lot of my life, and I hope you are pleased. Through these pages, I hope you have learned more interesting things about me than you knew before. I was a silly fun-loving kid, who regressed to an underachieving student after my Daddy died. It wasn't his fault, but when my life coach left me, I wasn't mature enough to continue down the path he suggested for me. I didn't talk to Mama about how I felt; I just simply gave up on the dream. There was a time in my life when, just like you, I thought my parents were the goofiest people alive. It was only when I became an adult that I fully recognized just how clever they were.

You have reached the end of the first half of my life in these pages, and if you think you've read a story about me, Georgia Patrice Kissentaner, you've missed something. This is not a story about me. It is a narrative about a few people, places, things and ideas that have shaped me. More importantly, it's about who has kept me. I'm not a religious fanatic, I simply acknowledge God for being who He is in my life.

He's always been my coach, but most of the time, I didn't pay attention. He's blown whistles in my life to call fouls, but I didn't hear them. I kept right on doing what I pleased. He gave me opportunities to shine, and I did, with little or no mention of Him. Most of the time, I took the fast breaks in life, and slam dunked, standing there waiting for the crowds to cheer. Few did. Other times, I have been guilty of waiting "in the lane" for others to do the right thing. Here was another violation on my record. That's okay, because in every basketball game, there is a halftime, and it's from this halftime in my life, that the coach has spoken to me. I have rested up, and drank some ***free water***, and am preparing myself for the next half.

Look at this. He's the same God who protected me in my twenties, the years of fears and learning. I call the twenties the years of fears because although I was an adult, I was still afraid of the unknown. I was still pretty immature, too. The *yearning* to be able to make my own decisions and do as I pleased directed every move I made. A bad college relationship took its toll on me, while I thought I was old enough to make a good decision. Like many other twenty-something adults, I made plenty of dumb choices. No matter what I try to teach you, you will make your fair share of bad decisions in your twenties. Hopefully, you will learn from them, just like I did. Always remember, it's no longer a mistake, if you learn a valuable lesson from it.

The same God loved me and came to my rescue in my thirties, the years of tears and *learning*. As a result of some bad decisions made in my twenties, I shed my fair share of tears during my early thirties. I had to learn what to say, and how to say it; where to go and who to go with. I had to grow up and learn how to be accountable for my actions.

However, at halftime, the tears seem to be drying up, and I'm preparing for the years of cheers, my forties. I anticipate the years of *earning,* which are just around the corner. I'm not living for financial wealth, but spending these good years living a rich life with my family, all healed from our injuries.

As your sole biological parent, I pray that I am living my life in such a way that you will know what to do, and what not to do as an adult. I spent so much of my meaningful time doing meaningless, trifling things that I can never undo, with people who will never mean as much to me, as the two of you do. I realized when Jordan spoke to Big Mama about the color of your father's casket, just how important you both are to me. You are both tasked with picking my casket, when I die. I want that decision to be one that reflects your love for me. Hopefully, I won't get a used crate and a pillow off your sofa.

As you embark on exciting lives as pre-teens, teens and then adulthood, I leave you with the following life lessons I've learned the hard way. Although I can never prevent the inevitable mistakes that come with growing up, I can only encourage you to remember who you are, and strive to make good mature decisions. I may not live to see you graduate high school or college, but I want you to hear my heart in the following lines, as I speak to your mind, body and soul.

Guard your mind.

1. Always seek Godly wisdom. Rely on those who have timely wisdom to assist you with your needs. Would you ask a two-year-old to teach you to drive? Case closed.

2. When you had no one else, you had each other. December 25, 2000. You were all each other had for almost thirty-five hours, until I could get there. You survived against the odds. Don't ever let anyone penetrate the ties you share as sisters.

3. Self-respect is the foundation for self-confidence. Love you for who you are. There's not another one like you, anywhere else.

4. Always respect those in authority over you. This includes me, your step dad, grandparents, aunts and uncles, teachers, supervisors at work, respective spouses and your minister.

5. Accept responsibility for your actions. If you mess up, fess up. Don't make excuses; make a difference.

6. Respect money.

7. Enjoy life with healthy moderation.

8. Like Aunt Thelma, use your "good dishes." The tragic irony in your father, your Aunt Jane and Uncle Reuben is that neither of them lived to be fifty years old. My hope is that they weren't waiting for "the right time" to use their good dishes.

9. Nurture your spirit of adventure, but do so with a purpose and a plan. Travel. Try new foods. Learn two foreign languages before you die. Ebonics doesn't count.

10. Be cautious of what you listen to and who you listen to. Do you realize that you both answer to your names because that's what I kept calling you as children? I called you Jordan, and the other Jamie, for so long, you now believe that those are your names. That's all you've heard, so that's all you know. What if your real names are Lupe and Margarita? How would you know? You wouldn't. So make sure the things you choose to listen to are good for your mind. We believe a lot of what we hear, and even more of what we see. Be careful.

11. Distance yourself from any negative influences around you. Feed your mind positive thoughts and you will see how much easier it is to approach difficulties.

12. Everyone you know right now is not everyone you will know later. Remember my supportive cast and other team members from the beginning of the book? Many of them quit playing; some switched teams, and others died. Keep your options open. Don't limit

yourself to your current surroundings. My new team mates weren't picked by me. This time, the Coach has sent them to me. One is a former cocaine user. (The Weekend Girls would have never associated with such a person.) One is a Pentecostal. (I didn't understand their worship practices.) One is Jewish. (I have learned that she has more soul than a lot of black Baptists I know.) One is a former neighbor, whom I had never made myself acquainted. Thirteen years later, we are as close as sisters. And of course, your step-dad looked nothing like the men I was familiar with. Once again, I didn't pick him, The Coach did.

13. People are watching you all the time. Make sure what they see represents the real you.

14. As your granny has told you, I'll remind you, "Pretty is as pretty does." Look your best all the time. Take pride in your appearance. Don't waste your money on French manicure. We're not wealthy enough to pay to have our nails polished to look like they aren't polished. ***When water was free, a getting your nails done meant they were polished bright red. Not so, today. Give me color, or give me my money back!***

15. Most people are good, and have good motives. Don't make a life of trying to prove how good you are. When it's in you, it'll show up. When it's not, it can't. A tree is known by the fruit it bears, according to the gospel of Matthew. Quoting Reverend Alton R. McKinley, "God has not called us to judge others, (Matthew 7:1-5) he has; however, commissioned us to

be fruit inspectors. You don't have to climb a lemon tree to know it's a lemon tree. You can see the lemons way be fore you reach the tree."

16. Never tie yourself to someone who is incapable of returning love to you. You deserve better.

17. You can't save the world. You can only make a positive difference in the world around you. Make every day you live count for something good.

18. Be a great friend. Your grandfather showed me an effective model for friendship, which I encourage you to adopt. He was honest with me at all times. He looked out for my well-being, and unselfishly gave his time to me.

19. There will always be people into whose mold you don't necessarily fit. That's okay; matter of fact, that's good. Everyone is different. Don't create a revolt, create results.

20. Keep saying "please" and "thank you". Yes Ma'am/Sir. This was required when I grew up, and I will require the same of you.

When water was free, "nigger" was a racial slur. Today, it is an awkward term of endearment. There are so many other words that could convey your loyalty or friendship to someone. Pick one, please.

21. Never place a pre-conceived value on friendship. If you place it too high, you'll become easily disappointed. Place it too low, and you'll settle for a poor-quality friendship.

22. When you find yourself in a friendship or relationship where you are doing more giving, than receiving, it's time to re-assess the relationship. In order to maintain healthy vibrant relationships, both parties must contribute equally. A one-sided, stagnant relationship cannot flourish.

23. In any relationship, establish rules and expectations early. One of my greatest heartbreaks came when I broke the rules of a relationship, which I didn't know existed. (I was nominated "mother of the group" and when I did as I thought the role suggested, things went awry.)

    a. Tell the truth, doing so in love.

    b. Do things expecting nothing in return.

    c. Be there for your friends, in the way they expect. (You do this by knowing what the rules are.)

    d. The minute you feel uncomfortable in any relationship, speak up. Make your concerns known. Hoping the situation will correct itself will not solve the situation. The Bible teaches about dealing with offenses and offenders. And if after following those steps, the issue is not resolved, it's okay to cut the ties. It's often one of the most difficult things to do, but it's okay. Life goes on.

24. Dream your dreams; not my dreams for you. It's only natural that parents want what's best for their children, however; just because I may suggest a direction in life for you, if it doesn't relate to what you want, you'll never enjoy it with the same zeal you would have, if it had been your desire. We may disagree from time to time, and just because I'm mom, it doesn't always mean I'm right. (Most of the time it does, but not always.) I'm still your parent, but I'll become your friend when you reach adulthood.

Respect your body.

25. You have a beautiful gift from God, which is not associated with your looks, intellect or athleticism. It's your virginity. Keep it until you have a husband. Sure, you'll be labeled a square or a shrew, but that's okay. I've been praying for godly husbands for you since you were born. When the man who God has prepared for you arrives...after he's bought the ring, and you both have filed for the license, and said "I do" and cut the cake...then do what is reserved for husbands and wives, in that order, please.

26. Guard yourself against those who will flatter you with flowery words and sweet nothings. When he tells you, "I think you are cute," kindly remind him, "According to scripture, the Bible says I am "fearfully and wonderfully made." (Psalm 139:14)

27. Because you are fearfully and wonderfully made, you don't have to settle for anything. Your grandfather was adamant about me not being a "that'll do negro." I, therefore, don't expect any less from you.

28. Maintain your standards of Godly living. In this, I'm saying that you are far too beautiful and intelligent to be any man's other woman. You've seen first-hand how playing this role can destroy a home. You have a choice in this matter. Choose the right way. Don't go looking for a man, because it has been said, "Whoso findeth a wife, finds a good thing." Not the other way around. Be still, be quiet, be patient, and let him find you.

29. Though a man may appear to be the answer to your prayers, remember this one thing: God will not send you someone who belongs to someone else. There are no strings attached. God won't have you sneaking around to be with this man; meeting up with him under the fateful cover of darkness. You won't have to find a male friend, call his number, and patch you through on the three-way. That's not God; that's straight from the evil one.

30. If you ever find yourself in such a relationship, remember this: It's very unlikely that he will ever leave his wife for you. He may possibly move out, and make alternate living arrangements, but not necessarily for you. Don't hold your breath. He's a free man, running wild. I've seen it on more than two occasions; he'll only stay with you until he finds someone else to "spoon up to" at night. Save yourself

the heartache. You can never forget the trademarked slogan of Pastor Terry M. Turner. "God don't bless no mess." (For the record, he is the conferee of two master's degrees, and has a great command of the English language, but illustrates his point, in a vernacular that even the youngest congregant doesn't miss it.) That's what makes him the best pastor, this side of heaven.

31. Continue eating right and exercising. (You're already off to a great start.)

32. Keep up the drug-free tradition. At age thirty-seven, I still have never experimented smoking marijuana, crack, or the other drugs. Unless you two drive me to try it during your high school years, I think I'm past the stage of peer pressure or giving in. (Of course alcohol is a drug, and I do drink wine, occasionally.) Ooops. One for the road…

When water was free, crack was what you didn't step on, because it may break your mama's back.

Nourish your soul.

33. Don't let anyone try and measure your salvation. You have confessed and believe Jesus to be the son of God, and God raised Him from the dead on the third day. That's it. Salvation is yours. You can't be kinda saved, just like you can't be kinda pregnant. Either you are or you're not. It's just that simple. Speaking in tongues, prophecy, and healing are spiritual gifts,

just as hospitality, helps and administration are gifts as well. Don't allow anyone to tell you that you have to have a certain gift in order to prove that you are saved. You have the gift of the blood of Jesus shed for your sins.

34. Go to church. No, it's not required, but it's the best way to be fed real soul food. No sense in starving yourself.

35. Don't hang on to the guilt of yesterday's mistakes. God promises new mercies every day. Feast on them.

36. Your appearance, attitude and aptitude can only get you so far, but by the grace of God, you are who you are (1Corinthians 15: 10).

37. When you are unable to figure out just what to do, try Proverbs 3:5-6. You may think you have all the answers and can explain your way through anything, but these scriptures can help you when nothing else makes sense. These few words helped me make it through the days following your recovery.

38. Forgive. Forgive. Forgive. I can never say it enough. Let go of the dead weight of grudges. They only slow you down and impede your growth progress. It may not be easy the first few times you do it, but like anything else, it becomes easier with practice. There are those who you will find it difficult to forgive, but do it anyway. Don't try to understand. Your job is to forgive and move on. There are a few people I've had

to forgive, and afterward, life was a little more pleasant.

39. Always remember the best in every situation, no matter how bad it may seem. I still remember how relieved I was to see you both after the accident.

40. Never forget just how much you loved your dad. He was a wonderful father to both of you and a great provider for our family. The only thing your dad was guilty of was disappointing me. And I'm over it. I encourage you to recall all the good times he shared with us, but the few difficulties I encountered with him, I've used as lessons in life.

41. I had forgotten how much I loved my daddy, until I wrote this book. But it was fun remembering your dad and my dad. Recently, I found out that earlier in his life, long before meeting Mama, he served time for murder! Yes, my daddy, a convicted murderer. But ya know what? After getting over the initial shock of Mama's confession to me, it didn't matter. He was my daddy.

42. I've forgiven the nameless woman mentioned in the book, and you should, too. She's taught me how to be a better prepared wife. Some of the most valuable knowledge I have ever gained, she has taught me and I must share it with you. I pray that when you both become married women, you won't have to experience the phone call like I did. In case you do, here's what your mother suggests:

43. Be prepared. (Other women will have a plan for your man, which excludes you.) Most of the time, other women like talking to married men about their personal problems with their own boyfriends. What they fail to realize is the married man probably has more issues in his own life than he can handle. Therefore, he can be of no assistance to help the situation. Also, the single woman certainly can't fix a married man's issues. By the way, a single woman should not maintain a friendship with a married man, without being friends with his wife first.

44. Be strong. (Stand firm on your convictions and lovingly demand that he comply with your wishes. Let him know you are happy to assist him with stopping the relationship, within the bounds of the law, ladies, okay?)

45. Be a wife. (Remember, what it took to get him, is what it takes to keep him. I'll tell you about that later, like at your wedding shower.)

46. Be protective. When another woman calls your home to start some mess, kindly stop her before she gets started. Let her know, "Thanks, but it's not necessary. We talked about it and everything is fine." (Even if it's not, it's still none of her business.) Not only have your nipped her program in the bud, you will have thrown a wrench into her program. Maintain your position and remember she's called you usually for no other reason than to mess with your mind. Do yourself a favor. Stay calm, and remember the Diva's rule number one. Never let them (anyone) see you sweat.

47. Don't make it a practice of telling your business to everyone, including your friends. Some people thrive on hearing how bad off you are, especially if they are lonely and unhappy. Secondly, if you and your mate are fortunate to resolve the matter, your friends will never forget. This makes a great topic of conversation when you are not around.

48. Even though contemporary wedding ceremonies now resemble a pick up basketball game, with "his side" and "her side", don't forget the referee — the one, who stood between you two, as you made the promises to love, honor and keep each other until death. If the actual minister who counseled and married you is not available, find one whom you both trust. Not someone who will take your side.

I love you too much to lie to you. Well, okay other than the Santa Claus thing, but other than that, it's true. -And look at how you found out the truth about Santa. The day when your daddy was called home to heaven, you found out the truth, as you both lay in our bed with the bedroom door cracked open, watching us put your gifts under the tree. See, the secret things belong to the Lord, but in His time, all things will be revealed.

For now, you see, all the lessons I've learned, all the strides I have yearned, and the gains yet to be earned began when water was free.

Dear Readers,

This is only the tip of the iceberg. If you would like to request Patrice K. Walker as a speaker at your seminars, workshops, lectures and retreats, and share more in her memories of the simpler life, you should contact her publicist, Valencia McClure at:

SimDen Publishing
1515 Town East Blvd
Suite 138-104
Mesquite, TX 75150
Or via e-mail Valencia@pkwalker.com

Please log on to www.pkwalker.com to become a member of our newsletter list.

Here's what's next with SimDen Publishing:

The Free Water Companion Journal, to be released fall 2004. Start journalizing your thoughts to share with your children, spouse, fiancée, friends or support group; available only through the author's website: www.pkwalker.com

Life Quest Retreats "Looking Back, Taking Stock and Moving Forward." In conjunction with Touchstone International, The SimDen Group will offer three-day retreats to focus on assessing your personal life; where you've been, where you are, and where you aspire to go. These scripturally reinforced retreats focus on purpose, passion and principles, for individuals and small groups.

The quarterly retreats are held in Dallas, Texas, and there will be one seminar at sea, each year. —Winter 2004

Family and Friends Cruise. Readers and their families will join the author and her family on a cruise, to celebrate family, love and free water. —Summer 2005

"**More Than Conquerors**" a national search for twelve women who despite the odds, have survived difficulties, and want to share their stories. —Fall 2005

All supplemental information is available at the author's web site, www.pkwalker.com.

Thank you so much for purchasing and reading When Water Was Free. If it has been a blessing to you, please tell somebody.

Remember, the best things in life are still free: love, family and water.

The Lord bless thee and keep thee:
The Lord make his face shine upon thee,
and be gracious unto thee:
The Lord lift up his countenance upon thee,
and give thee peace.
Numbers 6:24-26

Printed in the United States
20421LVS00001B/286-447